Pro
TEAC

By the same author

Problems in Plant Physiology
 (Students' and Teachers' Editions)

M. K. Sands

Problems in Animal Physiology

TEACHERS' EDITION

John Murray Albemarle Street London

© M. K. Sands 1975

First published 1975
Reprinted 1976

All rights reserved. No part of this publication may be reproduced, stored in a retrieval system, or transmitted, in any form or by any means, electronic, mechanical, photocopying, recording or otherwise, without the prior permission of John Murray (Publishers) Ltd., 50 Albemarle Street, London, W1X 4BD.

Set by H. Doust Art and Advertising Ltd., London
Printed Offset Litho in Great Britain by
Cox and Wyman Ltd., London, Fakenham and Reading

0 7195 3202 7

Using this book

In conjunction with practical work

In recent years school biology has moved from a descriptive approach to one involving more analysis and experimental work than before. But because of the pressure of time, or lack of money or facilities, a teacher can rarely do with a class all the experimental work he would wish, and data for analysis is not always easy to come by in the rush of a school term. The problems in this book present data and information in the areas usually taught in animal physiology at Advanced level, together with questions involving analysis and interpretation of the data. Where a student cannot gather his own data at first-hand during practical work, or if his experiment goes wrong, a problem analysing other people's results can substitute to a certain extent. Even with class practicals a problem can give a student guidance on how to analyse his own data.

As part of the theory

In theory work, modern biology frequently demands that statements should be substantiated by the evidence on which they are based. Some of these problems give such evidence and they could be used as an integral part of an exposition lesson, with verbal answers from the students contributing to the development of the topic.

Objectives

Apart from passing on information, a teacher will have in mind other objectives for a biology course. In addition, some biology syllabuses now include with the usual list of biological topics a statement of objectives covering scientific thinking and giving an indication of the abilities a student should have. He is expected not only to have a knowledge of the content of biology and to be able to remember and communicate it, but also to be able to formulate and assess hypotheses, analyse data, devise experiments, and draw and evaluate conclusions. The problems here can be used to teach such abilities and give practice in them. Indeed, some give data which one would not normally expect to find in an Advanced level course so that, with unfamiliar material, the student cannot use his memory to answer questions which ask him to think something out for himself.

Examinations

Such a syllabus, as well as others which do not list objectives, lead to examinations which include problem-type questions testing scientific thinking where candidates are asked to comment on information given at the start of the question. Because of their length and the mass of data they may contain, such questions can look formidable to a student unused to them. In actual fact, they can be quicker to answer and yield higher marks than the traditional essay-type questions, but a student does not realise this until he has tried a number during his course. The problems in this book can serve as useful practice for the problems section of an examination paper, and also as a source of ideas for school tests and examinations.

Using the problems

Within each chapter the problems differ in length and difficulty, and cover different content areas and abilities. It is not intended that a student should work through all the problems one after another, but that those which best serve a teacher's purpose should be chosen. Once selected, they can be integrated into the teaching in a number of ways. They could be given for homework before or during the development of a topic, or as an exercise in class at a particular stage of the work, or be used to stimulate group discussion. It is useful to work through a problem oneself before giving it to a class: unwanted questions can be omitted, or the problem can be otherwise tailored to the ability, time and interests of a class. The marking of problems is usually easier than essay marking, but, as with essays, problems benefit from class discussion of the answers after they have been done. Such a discussion can, if wanted, lead on to further hypotheses, open-ended experiments, reading or essay writing.

Acknowledgments

I am grateful to the following authors and publishers who have allowed me to make use of their material.

Figs. 1, 41A, 42, 49, 53: photographs by John Haller, Harris Biological Supplies.

Page 5: table from Haldane, J.S. and Priestley, J.G., (1905), 'The Regulation of the Lung Ventilation', p.249. *J. Physiol.* 32, 225-266.

Pages 9, 11: tables from Knut Schmidt-Nielsen, *Animal Physiology,* 2nd ed. Copyright (1964), pp. 33 & 34. By permission of Prentice-Hall, Inc., Englewood Cliffs, New Jersey.

Fig. 6 and *Page* 14 (table): from Hughes, G.M., (1963), *Comparative Physiology of Vertebrate Respiration,* Table 3. Heinemann Educational Books Ltd. Data of Fry and Hart, 1948.

Figs. 15, 17, 59, 60 and *Page* 17 (table): from Ganong, W.F. (1973), *Review of Medical Physiology,* 6th ed. Figs. 32-15, 35-10, 8-6, Table 30-1. Lange Medical Publications.

Pages 21, 54 (table): from Baldwin, E., (1962), *The Nature of Biochemistry,* Tables 3, 6. Cambridge University Press.

Fig. 16: from Chapman, G., (1967), *The Body Fluids and their Functions,* Fig. 4-5. Edward Arnold. Based on Redfield, A.C., (1934), 'The Haemocyanins', *Biol. Rev.,* 9, 175-212.

Figs. 19, 21: from Tanner, J.M., (1962), *Growth at Adolescence,* 2nd ed., Figs. 4, 2. Blackwell Scientific Publications, Ltd.

Fig. 22: from Harrison, G.A., Weiner, J.S., Tanner, J.M., and Barnicot, N.A., (1964), *Human Biology,* from Fig. 14. The Clarendon Press, Oxford.

Fig. 23: from Lippold, O.C.J., and Winton, F.R., (1968), *Human Physiology,* 6th ed., Fig. 32.5. Churchill Livingstone. After Lyon.

Fig. 24: from Stewart, C.P. and Dunlop, D.M., (1964), *Clinical Chemistry in Practical Medicine,* 6th ed., Fig. 20. Churchill Livingstone.

Page 35: table from Jensen, A.R., (1969), 'How much can we boost I.Q. and scholastic achievement', *Harvard Ed. Rev.,* 39, 1-123, table on p.49. Copyright 1969 by President and Fellows of Harvard College.

Page 36: table from Shields, J., (1962), *Monozygotic Twins,* Table 6. Oxford University Press.

Fig. 32: from Bollman, J.L., Mann, F.C., and Magath, T.B., (1924), 'Studies in the physiology of the liver, VIII. Effect of the total removal of the liver on the formation of urea', Fig. 5. *Amer. J. Physiol.,* 69, 371-392.

Page 52: Table from Bell, G.H., Davidson, J.N., and Emslie-Smith, D., (1972), 'Textbook of Physiology and Biochemistry', 8th ed., Table 32.7. Longman Group Ltd.

Fig. 34, *page* 56 (table): from Baldwin, E., (1964), *An Introduction to Comparative Biochemistry*, Fig. 1, and table on page 31. Cambridge University Press.

Fig. 35: photograph by M.I. Walker, from transparency set TPI, Harris Biological Supplies.

Page 61: table from Squires, B.T., (1953), 'Human salivary amylase secretion in relation to diet', p.155. *J. Physiol.*, 119, 153-6.

Fig. 37: photographs by Oxfam.

Figs. 38, 39: Hopkins, F.G., (1912), 'Feeding experiments illustrating the importance of accessory factors in normal dietaries', Figs. 4 and 2. *J. Physiol.*, 44, 425-460.

Page 67 (2nd table): from City of Birmingham Public Health Department.

Page 74: table from Baldwin, E., (1963), *Dynamic Aspects of Biochemistry*, Table 15. Cambridge University Press.

Figs. 41B and 41C, 55: photographs by J.H. Kugler, from transparency set EMI, Harris Biological Supplies.

Page 92: table from Anrep, G.V., (1920), 'Pitch discrimination in the dog', Table IV. *J. Physiol.*, 53, 367-385.

Fig. 56: from Hurry, S.W., (1965), *The Microstructure of Cells*, Fig. 12.6. John Murray.

I wish to record my thanks to S.W. Hurry and R.A. Hull for their comments on the problems and also to the following teachers and their sixth form students who tackled the problems in their initial form.

P. H. Holway	St. Dunstan's College, Catford
J. E. Maudsley	King Edward VI Camp Hill School for Girls, Birmingham
D. G. Mackean and D. Cuckney	Sir Frederic Osborn School, Welwyn Garden City
I. Sexton	Lincoln School
A. A. Radermacher	St. Paul's Boys' School, London

Cover: photograph by John Haller, Harris Biological Supplies.

Contents

Page numbers in brackets refer to the Teachers' Notes

1 Gas Exchange and Respiration

1.1	Lung capacity	2	[102]
1.2	Control of breathing	4	[102]
1.3	Adaptations to high altitude	5	[103]
1.4	Diving mammals	7	[103]
1.5	Measurement of metabolic rate	8	[103]
1.6	Calculation of basal metabolic rate	8	[104]
1.7	Metabolic rate and size	9	[104]
1.8	Oxygen consumption and activity	10	[105]
1.9	Oxygen consumption and temperature	11	[105]
1.10	Oxygen consumption in water	13	[105]
1.11	Respiratory quotient	14	[106]

2 Blood System

2.1	Origin of heart beat	16	[107]
2.2	Blood vessels	17	[107]
2.3	Capillary circulation	18	[108]
2.4	Foetal circulation in man	20	[108]
2.5	Blood pigments	21	[108]
2.6	Oxygen carriage	22	[109]
2.7	Dissociation curves	24	[109]
2.8	The transport of carbon dioxide	25	[109]
2.9	Blood groups	26	[110]
2.10	Inheritance of blood groups	28	[110]

3 Growth and Reproduction

3.1	Growth in humans	29	[111]
3.2	Thyroid action	31	[112]
3.3	Nature and nurture	33	[112]
3.4	Control of menstrual cycle	38	[115]
3.5	Ovulation and temperature	41	[115]
3.6	Gametogenesis	43	[116]
3.7	Artificial insemination	44	[116]
3.8	Reproductive behaviour	45	[116]
3.9	Hatching and temperature	46	[117]
3.10	Growth-controlling products in tadpoles	46	[117]
3.11	Metamorphosis in frogs	47	[118]
3.12	Litter size and survival	49	[118]

4 Excretion

4.1	Urea production and excretion	51	[119]
4.2	Nitrogenous excretion in man	51	[119]
4.3	Nitrogenous excretion in vertebrates	52	[119]
4.4	The kidney in bony fish	55	[120]
4.5	Regulation of body fluids in four invertebrates	55	[120]
4.6	Contractile vacuoles in protozoa	57	[121]

5 Nutrition

5.1	Executives, alcohol and coffee	60	[122]
5.2	Diet and amylase activity	60	[122]
5.3	Energy requirements	61	[122]
5.4	Milk and diet	64	[123]
5.5	Beri-beri	65	[124]
5.6	Fluoride and tooth decay	66	[124]
5.7	The production of veal	68	[124]

6 Digestion

6.1	Control of gastric secretion	70	[126]
6.2	Control of pancreatic secretion	72	[126]
6.3	The digestion and absorption of fat	73	[126]
6.4	Digestion of cellulose	74	[127]
6.5	Structure and function of the intestine and alveoli	75	[127]
6.6	Enzyme action under different conditions	77	[128]
6.7	An enzyme experiment	78	[128]
6.8	The liver and blood sugar	79	[128]
6.9	Diabetes	81	[129]

7 Nerves and Muscles

7.1	Conduction in nerves	84	[130]
7.2	Nerve-muscle preparations	86	[130]
7.3	Neuromuscular transmission	89	[131]
7.4	Reflexes	90	[131]
7.5	Muscle contraction	92	[132]
7.6	Glycolysis in muscle	95	[132]
7.7	Rods and cones	96	[132]

Problems in Animal Physiology

1 Gas Exchange and Respiration

1.1 Lung capacity

In man the volume of air inspired per minute is normally about 6 dm^3, about 500 cm^3 per breath and twelve breaths a minute. The name given to the volume of air which moves into (and out of) the lungs with each breath is the **tidal volume**. Air in addition to the tidal volume, inspired with extra effort, is the **inspiratory reserve volume**, and that actively expelled after passively breathing out is the **expiratory reserve volume**. The air left in the lungs after this active expulsion is the **residual volume**. It cannot be breathed out. The term **vital capacity** is given to the greatest volume of air which can be expired after a maximal inspiratory effort. Vital capacity plus residual volume give the **total capacity** of the lungs. Vital capacity is often measured medically in lung investigations: certain diseases of lung, chest and heart reduce the vital capacity whereas athletes and people in good physical condition usually have a greater vital capacity than people who lead a sedentary life.

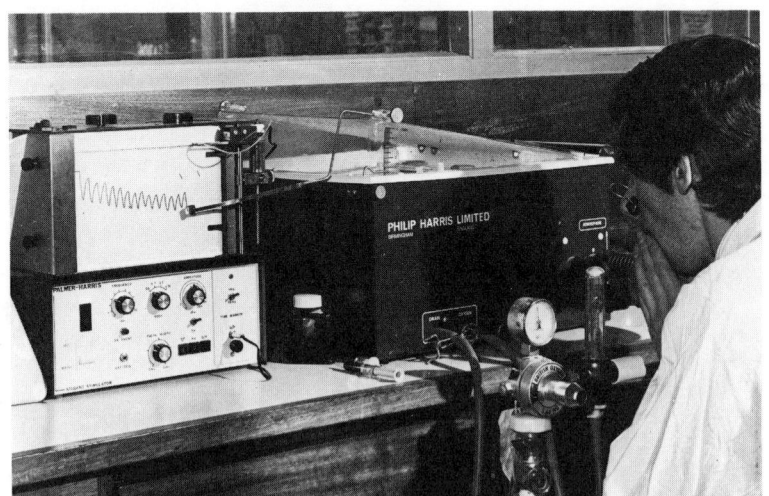

Fig. 1. **Spirometer**

(Photograph by John Haller, Harris Biological Supplies)

Gas Exchange and Respiration 3

All these volumes, except the residual volume, can be measured using a spirometer. The person breathes into and out of an oxygen-filled cylinder suspended in and over water. As he breathes out, the carbon dioxide he produces is absorbed. As he breathes in the cylinder goes down, the pen attached to it making a downward mark or trace on a kymograph. The reverse happens when he breathes out. Fig. 1 shows a spirometer.

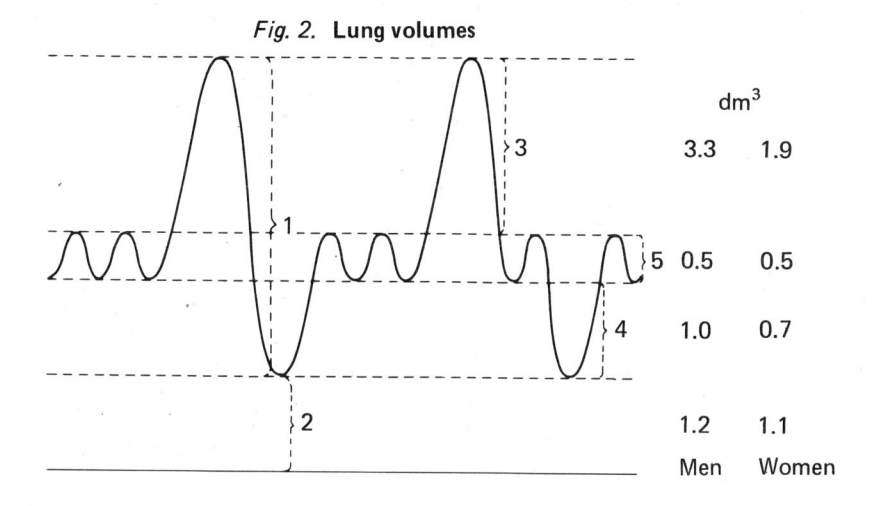

Fig. 2. Lung volumes

	dm^3	
	Men	Women
3	3.3	1.9
5	0.5	0.5
4	1.0	0.7
2	1.2	1.1

Fig. 2 is a diagram to show the volumes described above, giving also some indication of the average size of each volume. In order to give a base line representing a completely empty lung, the traces are upside down compared with the spirometer reading.

1 From the description above name 1 to 5 on Fig. 2.

2 What is the vital capacity for

   a a man

   b a woman?

3 What is the total capacity for

   a a man

   b a woman?

Fig. 3 (page 4) shows two spirometer tracings given by the same person. A is given at rest, B after strenuous exercise.

4 Calculate for this person

   a the number of breaths per minute at rest and after exercise

   b the average volume breathed in at rest and after exercise.

4   Gas Exchange and Respiration

Fig. 3. **Spirometer tracings**

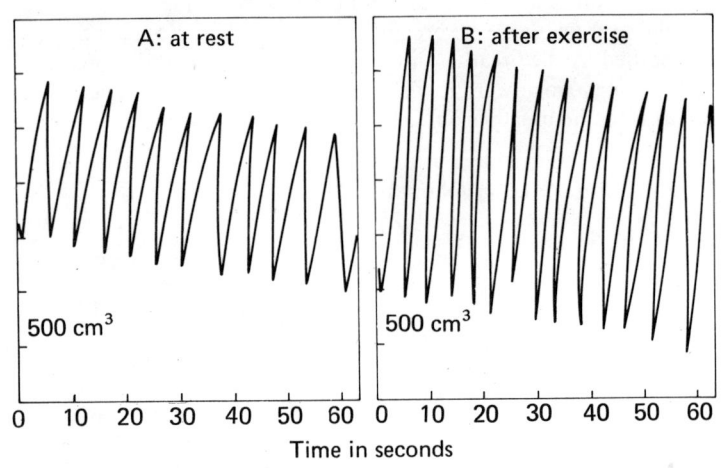

A: at rest

B: after exercise

500 cm^3

500 cm^3

Time in seconds

5 From these tracings what is the effect of exercise on breathing?
6 Why is the tracing moving downwards from left to right?
7 What precautions for the safety of the subject should be taken while using a spirometer to obtain tracings such as those above?

1.2   Control of breathing

There is about 21 per cent oxygen in normal air, and about 0.04 per cent carbon dioxide. The composition of inspired and expired air is shown in the table below.

Percentage composition of inspired and expired air

	Inspired air	Expired air	Air in lung alveoli
Oxygen	20.96	16.3	14.2
Carbon dioxide	0.04	4.0	5.5
Nitrogen and other gases	79.00	79.7	80.3

It is often thought that it is a shortage of oxygen in the air which makes us breathe faster, the result being the same amount of oxygen per unit time

Gas Exchange and Respiration

entering the pulmonary circulation. In fact, if the oxygen content of the air is reduced without increasing the amount of carbon dioxide, there is no change in breathing until the amount of oxygen falls from 21 per cent to about 13 per cent.

The second table shows the relationship between breathing and the amount of carbon dioxide in the air, in an investigation in 1905 using J.S. Haldane as the subject.

Breathing and the amount of carbon dioxide in inspired air

% carbon dioxide in inspired air	0.04	0.79	1.52	2.28	3.11	5.48	6.02
Average depth of respiration, cm^3	673	739	794	911	1232	1845	2104
Average number of breaths per minute	14	14	15	15	15	16	27
Volume breathed per minute, normal = 100	100	111	128	141	191	311	631
% carbon dioxide in alveolar air	5.6	5.5	5.55	5.8	5.5	6.8	6.6

1 What is the effect of an increased percentage of carbon dioxide in the inspired air on the rate and depth of breathing?

2 The increase of carbon dioxide in inspired air is not paralleled by a similar increase in the alveolar air. Suggest why.

3 When, in normal life, would you expect a similar increase in breathing to occur?

4 Which does this problem suggest controls the rate and depth of breathing, at least initially: oxygen or carbon dioxide?

1.3 Adaptations to high altitude

With increasing altitude, although the composition of the air stays the same, the total barometric pressure falls. The partial pressure of oxygen therefore also falls and there is less oxygen per unit volume of air than at sea level. As an example of the effect of this reduction on the availability of oxygen, the oxygen saturation of haemoglobin at 4300 m is only about 82 per cent as compared with the normal 95 per cent. To compensate, a person

6 Gas Exchange and Respiration

breathes faster. Between 2500 and 3000 metres a person will start to suffer from mountain sickness: he can no longer calculate accurately, there is a sense of elation and giddiness, together with headaches, irritability and nausea.

It is possible for a person who normally lives at or near sea level to become acclimatised to living at high altitudes. Over some weeks there is a gradual increase in the rate of ventilation, which persists for a little while after a return to sea level. Mountain dwellers have a greater lung volume and chest size than is normal at sea level.

1 Apart from those mentioned above, suggest two other adaptations to high altitude which, in spite of a reduced amount of oxygen in the air, would help to make available the required amount of oxygen to the tissues.

2 The number of red blood cells may have been one of your answers to question 1. The table gives the numbers of red blood cells per cubic millimetre of blood for man and some other animals at various heights. Comment on the figures.

	Altitude	Millions RBC mm^{-3}

Man:
    resident at
    permanent resident at
    temporary resident at
	sea level
	5400m
	5400m
		5.0
		7.37
		5.95

Sheep:
    at
    acclimatised at
    acclimatised at
	sea level
	3100m
	4700m
		10.5
		11.5
		12.05

Rabbit:
    at
    acclimatised at
	sea level
	5400m
		4.55
		7.00

Vicuna: an animal which lives at a high altitude:
    at
    at
	sea level
	4700m
		14.9
		16.6

1.4 Diving mammals

Diving mammals can stay under water for much longer periods of time than one would expect considering that they breathe by means of lungs. Man has a maximum diving time, without breathing apparatus, of only about two and a half minutes. Seals and beavers can stay under water for up to about fifteen minutes, and whales for 30 to 120 minutes or more.

How can diving mammals stay under water for so long? Their lungs are not specialised, being similar to those of other mammals. Indeed, they may even breathe out excess air before diving, becoming less buoyant. Neither can their hearts or brains do without oxygen for any longer than non-diving mammals. And although they do have more blood than non-divers, able to carry more oxygen, and more of the oxygen-storing myoglobin in their muscles, these differences are not enough to account for the length of time they can dive.

Below is a list of other observations about the physiology of seals during and after a dive. Put them together to give a brief account of some of the mechanisms which enable a seal to stay under water.

During a dive:

The flow of blood through the peripheral circulation (skin, muscles, flippers, and some other organs) is dramatically reduced by contraction of muscle in the walls of the arteries supplying them.

Oxygen consumption by the tissues from the oxygen supply in the blood falls to about one-third of normal.

The heart rate slows down considerably, but blood pressure in the main arteries remains normal as the volume of blood pumped from the heart stays about the same as normal.

Myoglobin in the muscle has given up most of its oxygen after five or six minutes; thereafter lactic acid rapidly accumulates in the muscle.

The amount of lactic acid in the blood remains normal, or increases only slowly later in the dive.

The amount of oxygen in the fully saturated blood falls steadily from the start of the dive to the end.

After a dive:

The peripheral circulation and heart rate return to normal.
Air is immediately taken into the lungs.
There is increased oxygen consumption by the tissues.
Lactic acid disappears from the muscle.
There is a great increase in the lactic acid content of the blood.

8 Gas Exchange and Respiration

1.5 Measurement of metabolic rate

Metabolism involves the use of energy to maintain the life processes of all organisms. A measure of cell respiration rate is, therefore, a good indication of general metabolic activity.

Respiration can be summarised:

$$\text{substrate} + \text{oxygen} \longrightarrow \text{carbon dioxide} + \text{water} + \text{heat}$$

It follows that respiration could, at least in theory, be measured by a decrease in the amount of substrate in the organism's body, the uptake or consumption of oxygen, the consumption of food, the production of heat, or the production of carbon dioxide.

1 Suggest experiments designed to measure in an animal or a plant
   a a decrease in the amount of substrate used for respiration
   b the uptake of oxygen
   c the amount of food eaten
   d the production of heat.

   Give any advantages or disadvantages of each method.

2 Although the metabolic rate of different animals, measured as rate of volume uptake of oxygen per unit body mass per hour, could be compared, the comparison can be invalid, for a number of reasons. Suggest three.

3 It isn't easy to measure the basal metabolic rate of animals other than man, as a true basal resting state cannot be forced on them. If you were asked to find out the metabolic rate of each of the organisms in the list below, which of the methods mentioned in question 1 would you use?

Mouse	Fish	Seeds
Elephant	Plant	

1.6 Calculation of basal metabolic rate

From the volume of oxygen consumed by a person it is possible to calculate the total energy production. Since oxygen is not stored and since its consumption in the resting stage always keeps pace with immediate needs, the volume of oxygen consumed per unit time is proportional to the energy liberated. The amount of energy released by 1000 cm^3 of oxygen varies slightly with the substrate (carbohydrate, fat or protein) being oxidised in the body, but the usual value of energy per 1000 cm^3 of oxygen is taken as 20.17 kilojoules (kJ).

To calculate the basal metabolic rate (BMR), the volume of oxygen used by the person at rest about twelve hours after the last meal is determined. In order to compare people of different size (to give a standard measure) the number of kJ produced is divided by the surface area of the person, and the final result, the BMR, is expressed as $kJ\,m^{-2}\,h^{-1}$. For an average twenty-year old man the BMR is 174.1, for a woman 151.9.

For a resting man who has a surface area of $1.9\,m^2$, using $300\,cm^3$ oxygen per minute, calculate

1 the BMR

2 the number of kilojoules of food to be eaten over twenty-four hours to maintain weight.

1.7 Metabolic rate and size

For the activities involved in metabolism to proceed, energy is needed, even when the animal is resting or asleep. One way of finding the metabolic rate of an animal is to measure the amount of oxygen used over a period of time. Larger animals will use more oxygen than smaller ones, so the results are usually expressed as the volume of oxygen consumed per unit body mass (cubic millimetres of oxygen per gram).

The table shows the metabolic rates of mammals of different body masses.

Metabolic rates of some mammals

	Body mass in kg	Oxygen consumption per hour in $mm^3\,g^{-1}$
Mouse	0.025	1580
Rat	0.226	872
Rabbit	2.200	466
Dog	11.700	318
Man	70.0	202
Horse	700.0	106
Elephant	3800.0	67

1 Using a log scale for both axes draw a graph of metabolic rate against body mass.

2 Describe the relationship between mass and metabolic rate for the animals in this list.

3 Suggest one reason, related to heat loss, to account for the fact that small mammals have a high metabolic rate.

If metabolic rate is expressed in terms of surface area instead of body mass, for example the number of kilojoules per square metre, a table such as that on page 10 is obtained. This shows a more constant relationship between metabolic rate and surface area, than between metabolic rate and mass.

10 Gas Exchange and Respiration

Daily intake and expenditure of energy for some mammals

	Needs kJ	Metabolic rate kJ kg^{-1}	kJ m^{-2}
Mouse	167	887	4 957
Dog	3 200	218	4 350
Man	8 800	134	4 360
Pig	10 500	80	4 495
Horse	21 000	46	3 976

4 How does this table support the view that heat loss and surface area are related?

5 A reptile with a mass of about one kilogram has a metabolic rate of only 9.2 kilojoules per kilogram day. Again relating your answer to body temperature, say why you think the reptile's metabolic rate is so low.

6 The data given above suggests that there is a theoretical minimum size for mammals. How?

7 A maximum size limit for mammals does not seem to be as clearly indicated on metabolic grounds as does the minimum size limit. However, terrestrial mammals do not now come much bigger than elephants. Suggest a reason for this.

8 What problems would face an elephant if it had a metabolic rate as high as that of a mouse?

1.8 Oxygen consumption and activity

The rate of oxygen consumption depends on the total metabolic activity of the organism. In an animal such activity varies from species to species according to the way of life. It also varies from time to time in an individual depending on its age, activity, and state of nutrition, and the time of day. For example, the squid consumes four times more oxygen per gram hour than the less active octopus; the mackerel which is an active and fast swimmer consumes twelve times more than the very sluggish puffer fish.

1 The relative uptake of oxygen is given in the table (page 11) for various animals at rest, showing a great deal of variation in metabolic rate from one animal to another. What trends do you notice?

Gas Exchange and Respiration 11

Oxygen uptake in some animals

	Relative oxygen uptake per hour
Sea anemone	1
Octopus	.6
Squid	25
Eel	10
Trout	17
Man	15
Mouse	120
Humming bird	270
Humming bird (flying)	3008

2 The volume of oxygen used is also an indication of how much food is being oxidised, and hence of how much the animal has to eat a day. Would a man or a mouse have to eat more, relative to body mass, per day?

3 Which of the two (man or mouse) will have the higher rate of breathing and heart beat? Why?

4 Fig. 4 shows the basal metabolism of girls up to twenty years. Comment on the variation with age.

Fig. 4. **Basal metabolism of girls**

BMR in arbitrary units

0 2 4 6 8 10 12 14 16 18 20
Age in years

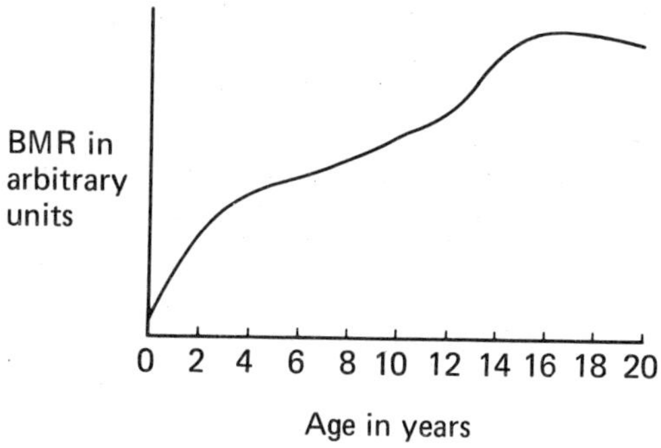

1.9 Oxygen consumption and temperature

Poikilotherms (cold-blooded animals) remain more or less at the same temperature as the air or water in which they live. Homoiotherms (birds and mammals) can keep their body temperature more or less constant, at a temperature suitable for activity.

12 Gas Exchange and Respiration

1 At an air temperature of 10 °C would you expect a poikilotherm or a homoiotherm to be the more active and why?

2 Say why you think
   a poikilotherms are sluggish or inactive during certain seasons of the year and at certain times of day or night
   b there can be a northern limit on the spread of some poikilotherms.

Fig. 5. **Oxygen consumption and temperature**

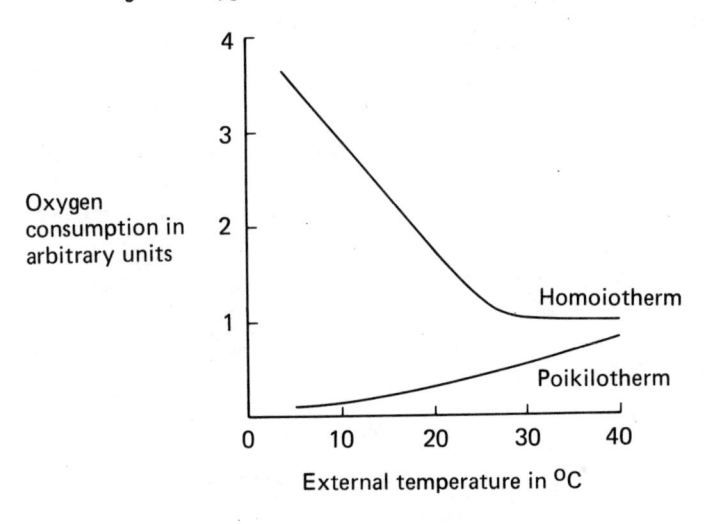

Oxygen consumption in arbitrary units

External temperature in °C

3 Fig. 5 shows the changes in oxygen consumption in a typical poikilotherm and homoiotherm with increasing temperature. Explain the increase in oxygen consumption in homoiotherms with decreasing temperature.

4 If the temperature of a special container which does not allow a mouse to move about is lowered from 30 °C to 20 °C, would you expect the heat given off by the mouse to increase or decrease? Why?

5 During hibernation the body temperature of a mammal is considerably below its normal temperature.
   a What do you expect to happen to the metabolic rate, and the heart and breathing rate during hibernation?
   b How are these changes adaptations to a cold climate?

1.10 Oxygen consumption in water

Unlike air-breathing animals, those living in water have to cope with the effect of temperature on the solubility of gases in their respiratory medium.

Fig. 6 shows the oxygen consumed by a fish at different temperatures, and the table shows the oxygen content of water at different temperatures.

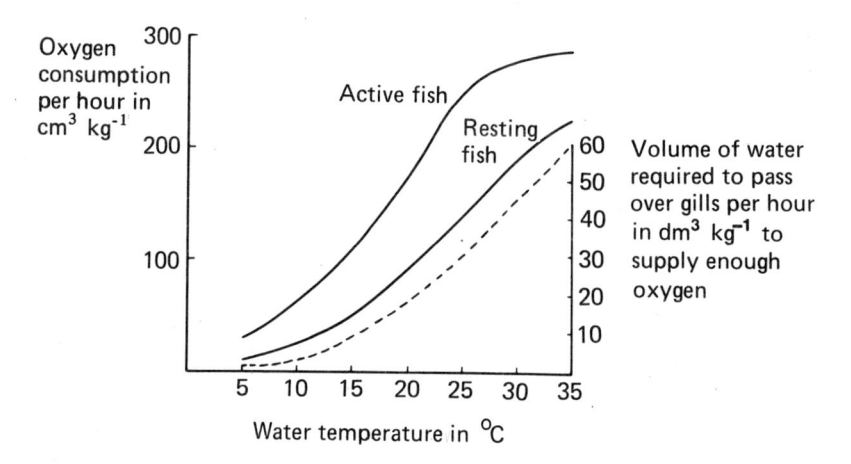

Fig. 6. **The effect of temperature on oxygen uptake by a goldfish**

Oxygen consumption per hour in cm^3 kg^{-1}

Active fish
Resting fish

Volume of water required to pass over gills per hour in dm^3 kg^{-1} to supply enough oxygen

Water temperature in °C

Temperature	Oxygen content of water in cm^3 dm^{-3}
5	9.0
15	7.0
25	5.8
35	5.0

1 What is the effect of increasing temperature on
   a the volume of dissolved oxygen in the water
   b the volume of oxygen needed by the fish, both resting and active?
2 What problem is posed to the fish as the temperature of the water rises?
3 How do you think the fish overcomes the problem?
4 When do you think the fish will start to be in difficulties with a rising temperature?

14　Gas Exchange and Respiration

5　The table below shows the volume of oxygen consumed per hour by a marine snail at different temperatures in sea water. The results are given in terms of grams flesh mass, without shells.

Oxygen uptake by a snail at different temperatures

Temperature in °C	Oxygen consumption per hour in mm^3 g^{-1}
5	28
10	32
15	35
20	52
25	96
30	108
35	79

Comment on these results.

1.11　Respiratory quotient

The respiratory quotient (RQ) of an organism indicates the type of foodstuff being used in respiration. It is of value in identifying metabolic adaptations. The RQ is the ratio of the volume of carbon dioxide produced by the organism to the volume of oxygen consumed, per unit time. The oxidation of a carbohydrate can be summarised:

$$C_6H_{12}O_6 + 6O_2 \longrightarrow 6CO_2 + 6H_2O$$
glucose + oxygen　　　　carbon dioxide + water

Thus the RQ is $\dfrac{CO_2 \text{ produced}}{O_2 \text{ consumed}} = \dfrac{6CO_2}{6O_2} = 1$

For one fat the equation is:

$$C_{57}H_{104}O_6 + 80\,O_2 \longrightarrow 57CO_2 + 52H_2O$$
triolein

Gas Exchange and Respiration 15

$$\text{which gives } RQ = \frac{57}{80} = 0.71$$

Other fats give similar figures.

Approximate RQs for the complete oxidation of respirable substances are:

Fats	0.7
Carbohydrates	1.0
Proteins and amino acids	0.9

These values are rarely obtained in practice because there is seldom complete oxidation. In addition proteins vary much in composition and are difficult to separate. In any case, a mixture of substances may be being used in respiration. An RQ slightly higher than 1.0 may indicate the conversion of carbohydrate to fat. The higher RQ is given as a result of the conservation of oxygen in the organic transformation. RQs of 2 to 7 suggest that anaerobic respiration is occurring.

Below are some RQ values for different organisms and tissues.

	RQ
Man, on an average mixed diet	0.8 – 0.85
Earthworm	0.75
Drosophila at rest	1.23
Drosophila during flight	1.0
Nerve tissue, resting	0.77
Brain	0.98
Geese, forced feeding with carbohydrates to fatten for market	1.4
Geese, basal diet	0.7
Paramecium	0.99

1 For each animal say what substrate(s) could be being metabolised.
2 The RQ is not necessarily constant throughout the life cycle of an animal. What could cause changes in the RQ?
3 The volume of carbon dioxide expired and oxygen inspired may vary with factors other than the food being used. For example, during exercise the RQ of a man may reach 2.0. After exercise it may fall for a while to 0.5. Explain these two figures.

2 Blood System

2.1 Origin of heart beat

The heart will continue to beat after all nerves to it have been cut.
The foetal heart starts to pulsate before any nerves have grown into it.
Under certain conditions the heart will beat alone, outside the body, for hours without outside stimulation.

1 What do these facts indicate about the origin of the heart beat?

It is possible to tie a thread between the sinus venosus and the atria of a frog's heart in what is called a first Stannius ligature. After tightening the ligature the sinus venosus carries on beating with the original rhythm, but the atria and ventricle stop for a time and then start beating with a new and different rhythm. When the sinus venosus of a tortoise heart is separated from the ventricle except for a narrow connecting bridge containing some atrial muscle and the nerve, the ventricle still beats in rhythm with the sinus venosus. If the nerve is cut there is no change, but if the connecting bridge of muscle is cut the ventricle either stops or beats with a new rhythm.

2 What seems to be the tissue which conducts the excitation wave from sinus venosus to ventricle?

Birds and mammals have a sinus venosus only in the embryonic heart. In the non-embryonic heart it is reduced to a small mass of modified muscle tissue called the sino-atrial node, located in the wall of the right atrium close to where the superior vena cava enters it.

If the sino-atrial node is heated or cooled, the heart rate is increased or slowed down correspondingly. Heating or cooling other parts of the heart has no effect on heart rate. Similarly, drugs alter the heart rate only when placed on the node. The action potential accompanying the contraction of heart muscle is first detected in the sino-atrial node. When William Harvey, in 1628, cut an excised heart in small pieces, he noted that each piece continued to beat by itself. However, the pieces from the atrium beat more quickly than those from the ventricle. Since then a definite gradient in beating speed of isolated portions has been observed from the sinus venosus to the apex of the ventricle.

3 Does this further evidence support the idea of the sino-atrial node as the pacemaker of the heart? If so, how?

There is a second node of modified muscle fibres, the atrio-ventricular node, at the base of the right atrium. Large muscle fibres (the Purkinje fibres) arise from it as the Bundle of His, which branches into two, one branch going to the right ventricle, the other to the left, each giving off numerous fine branches into the ventricular muscle. When either branch of fibres is cut, the ventricle served by that bundle stops beating, or beats with a different rhythm. The other ventricle continues to beat normally.

Fig. 7. **Diagrammatic section through the mammalian heart**

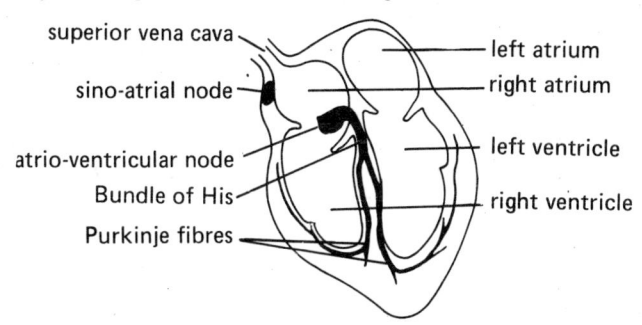

- superior vena cava
- sino-atrial node
- atrio-ventricular node
- Bundle of His
- Purkinje fibres
- left atrium
- right atrium
- left ventricle
- right ventricle

4 How does this evidence support the view that the Purkinje fibres conduct the excitation wave from the atrio-ventricular node to the ventricles?

2.2 Blood vessels

The table gives some of the characteristics of various types of blood vessels in man.

	Diameter of lumen	Thickness of wall	Total cross-sectional area for all vessels of each type, relative to aorta	Percentage of total blood volume contained in all vessels of each type
Aorta	25 mm	2 mm	1	2
Artery	4 mm	1 mm	4.5	8
Arteriole	30 μm	20 μm	89	1
Capillary	6 μm	1 μm	1000	5
Venule	20 μm	2 μm	890	
Vein	5 mm	500 μm	9	50
Vena cava	30 mm	1.5 mm	4	

18 Blood System

1 Comment on any relationships you observe in this table, and explain them as far as you can.

2 Explain the percentage of blood volume contained in the arterial system compared with the venous system.

3 The same volume of blood which leaves the heart returns to it, but the velocity at which blood flows through the system varies. The average velocity is inversely proportional to the total cross-sectional area of the part of the system the blood is in. Arrange these in order of the velocity you would expect: aorta, venule, capillary, vein.

4 Blood pressure varies with age and sex, but on average one can say that the pressure in the aorta rises to about 120 mmHg during systole (the contraction phase of the heart), and falls to about 70 mmHg during diastole (heart relaxed). Because systole is shorter than diastole the mean pressure is about 80 mmHg. How would you expect pressure to change in the vessels from aorta to vena cava?

5 The figure gives diagrammatic curves for total cross-sectional area, mean velocity of blood flow, and mean pressure, drawn to different scales. Say which curve is which.

Fig. 8. Cross-sectional area of vessels; velocity and pressure of blood flow

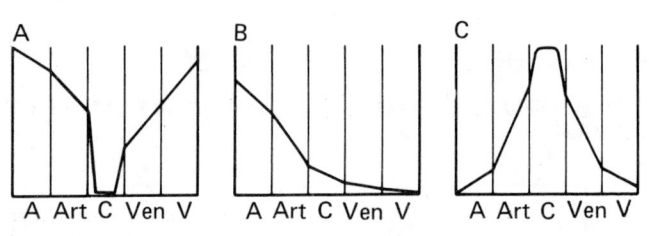

A Art C Ven V   A Art C Ven V   A Art C Ven V

A: arteries   Art: arterioles   C: capillaries   Ven: venules
V: veins

2.3 Capillary circulation

All the blood in the body can pass through the capillaries in a matter of minutes, even though flow through a capillary is so very slow. It is about 0.5 mm per second compared with 400 to 440 mm per second mean flow in the aorta, and 300 mm per second in veins.

Only five per cent of the circulating blood is in the capillaries at any one time, but this is the 'working end' of the circulation. It is across the capillary walls that oxygen and nutrients enter the interstitial tissue fluid, and carbon dioxide and waste products enter the blood. This exchange is essential to the survival of all the body tissues. It is said that a volume equal to the entire blood plasma volume enters and leaves the tissues every minute.

The capillary wall is a thin membrane of squamous epithelium cells. It allows all the contents of the blood plasma except most of the proteins to pass through it. This passage through the capillary walls depends on the nature of the wall and on the pressure of filtration. The pressure of filtration is what is left when the outward pressure of blood flow in the capillaries (the hydrostatic pressure of the blood) has been opposed by the tendency of the blood plasma to draw fluid in from the tissue fluid which has a lower osmotic pressure than the blood (OP blood minus OP tissue fluid), plus the pressure of the tissue fluid on the capillaries (hydrostatic pressure of tissue fluid).

The figure shows diagrammatically these pressures and opposing pressures in a capillary. The hydrostatic pressure (HP) of the blood, which differs at the two ends of the capillary, is opposed by the HP of the tissue fluid. The osmotic pressure (OP) of the blood plasma protein is opposed by the OP of the tissue fluids. The numbers are mmHg.

Fig. 9. **Pressures in and around a capillary**

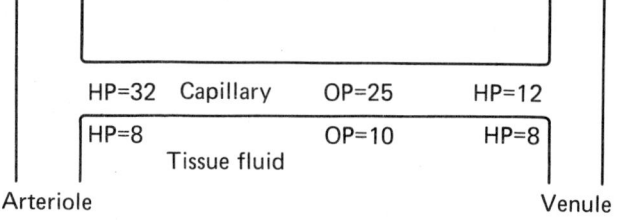

```
              HP=32   Capillary    OP=25        HP=12
              HP=8                 OP=10        HP=8
                      Tissue fluid
   Arteriole                                         Venule
```

1 What is the effective or net hydrostatic pressure of the blood in the capillary

   a at the arteriole end
   b at the venule end?

2 What is the effective osmotic pressure of the blood plasma?

3 What, therefore, is the filtration pressure at

   a the arteriole end of the capillary
   b the venule end of the capillary?

4 Which way, therefore, will fluid move at each end of the capillary?

5 Kwashiorkor is a condition common to people living on a diet which is adequate in calories but grossly deficient in protein. One of its characteristics is oedema: the accumulation of tissue fluid in abnormally

large amounts causing swelling. Fig. 37 shows a child suffering from kwashiorkor. Given that it is the proteins in the blood plasma which are largely responsible for its OP of 25 mmHg, suggest a reason for the oedematous condition in kwashiorkor.

2.4 Foetal circulation in man

Fig. 10 is a diagram of the blood circulation in a human foetus. The blood in the umbilical vein is about 80 per cent saturated with oxygen (compared with 98 per cent saturation in the arterial circulation of an adult). The saturation of the mixed blood in the inferior vena cava is about 67 per cent, of the aorta and umbilical arteries about 60 per cent, and of the portal and systemic venous blood about 26 per cent.

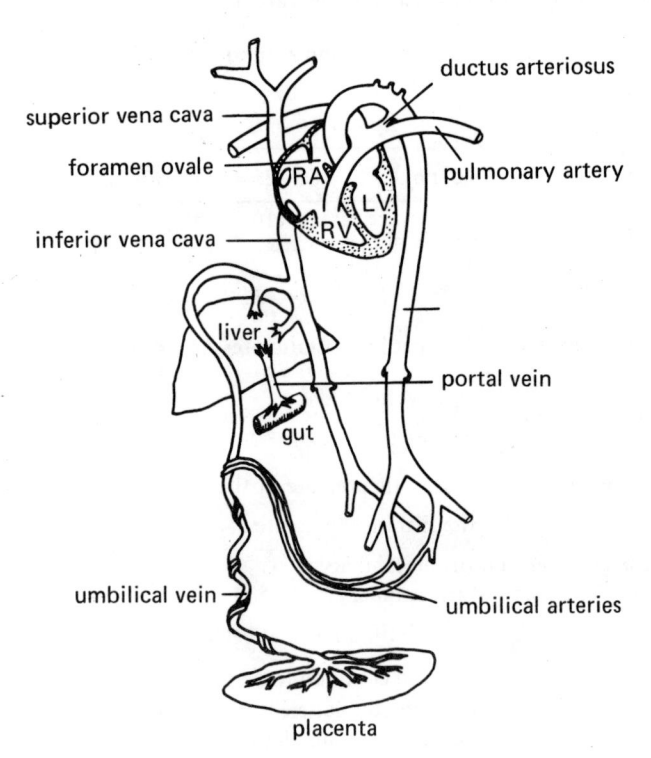

Fig. 10. **Foetal circulation**

1 Use arrows to show the direction of blood flow through this circulation.

After birth the blood passes through the lungs in the pulmonary circulation where it is oxygenated. This is not so in the foetus of course. Its lungs are collapsed and their resistance to blood flow is high.

2 From the diagram, where is most of the blood in the pulmonary artery of the foetus diverted to?

In the foetus oxygenated blood enters the right atrium, compared with the situation after birth where oxygenated blood enters the left atrium before it is sent round the body through the aorta.

3 What features of the foetal circulation allow oxygenated blood to enter the aorta?

4 What do you think happens at or shortly after birth to the two by-pass routes mentioned in your answers to questions **2** and **3**? What would be the possible effects of the circulation remaining as it was before birth?

2.5 Blood pigments

There are four main groups of respiratory pigments in the animal kingdom. All of them transport oxygen, with which they combine in a reversible reaction, from the respiratory surface to the tissues. They all increase the ability of the blood to take up and transfer oxygen, so that more oxygen per unit volume is carried than would be possible without them.

Respiratory pigments

	Molecules of oxygen to one atom metal	Pigment held in plasma or corpuscle	Oxygen cm^3 in 100 cm^3 of blood
Haemoglobin	1	Corpuscles	Mammals 25
			Birds 18.5
			Reptiles 9
			Amphibians 12
			Fish 9
		Plasma	Annelids 6.5
			Molluscs 1.5
Haemocyanin	½	Plasma	Molluscs 2
			Crustaceans 3
Haemerythrin	⅓	Corpuscles	Annelids 2
Chlorocruorin	1	Plasma	Annelids 9
Sea water	—	—	0.5

22 Blood System

The pigments have two parts, an active or prosthetic group, and a protein. In haemoglobin, the pigment of human blood, the prosthetic group which carries the oxygen is a complex iron compound called haem. The protein part is called globin

In the animal kingdom the four main groups of blood pigment are:

a haemoglobin, a red compound containing iron, found in vertebrates, some annelids, some molluscs
b haemocyanin, a blue compound containing copper, found in some molluscs, crustaceans
c haemerythrin, a red compound containing iron, found in some annelids
d chlorocruorin, a green compound containing iron, found in some annelids.

The table (page 21) shows some of the properties of the four pigments.

1 Compare the other three pigments with haemoglobin in relation to

   a the amount of oxygen carried per atom of metal
   b the amount of oxygen carried per 100 cm^3 blood.

2 How much do the pigments improve on the oxygen-carrying capacity of a body fluid something like sea water, with no pigment at all?

3 Suggest a reason for the greater oxygen-carrying capacity of vertebrate haemoglobin compared with invertebrate haemoglobin.

2.6 Oxygen carriage

In vertebrates, and also some invertebrates, oxygen is carried by the protein haemoglobin as an unstable compound, oxyhaemoglobin. Oxygen is rapidly picked up by the haemoglobin when the partial pressure of oxygen is high and rapidly released (unloaded) when the partial pressure is low. (The partial pressure of a gas is that part of the total pressure of air exerted in the air by the gas concerned). 100 cm^3 of blood, when 100 per cent saturated with oxygen, contain about 20.1 cm^3 oxygen.

Fig. 11, the oxygen-haemoglobin dissociation curve, gives the percentage saturation of haemoglobin at different partial pressures of oxygen, at pH 7.4 and 38 °C.

1 In the oxygenated blood of the pulmonary capillaries the partial pressure of oxygen is about 97 mmHg. In venous blood it is 40 mmHg, and in the tissues 5 to 30 mmHg.
   From the shape of the curve above discuss the effect the different partial pressures of oxygen have on the loading and unloading of the haemoglobin at various places in the body.

Blood System 23

Fig. 11. Oxygen haemoglobin dissociation curve

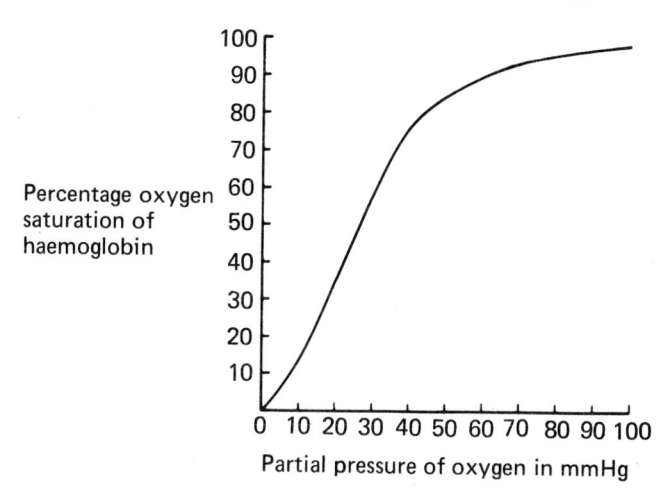

[Graph: Percentage oxygen saturation of haemoglobin (0–100) vs Partial pressure of oxygen in mmHg (0–100), showing sigmoidal curve]

2 Figs. 12, 13 and 14 show the effect of pH, temperature and the partial pressure of carbon dioxide on the dissociation of oxyhaemoglobin. In each case an increase in acidity, temperature or partial pressure of carbon dioxide moves the curve to the right.
For each set of curves consider the situation at a partial pressure of oxygen in the tissues of 20 mmHg. Say how the dissociation of oxyhaemoglobin is affected with an increase in each condition.

3 Of what value are these effects during exercise?

4 100 cm^3 arterial blood, 97 per cent saturated, contain 19.79 cm^3 oxygen. 100 cm^3 venous blood which is only 75 per cent saturated, contain 15.22 cm^3 oxygen. For a person with 4.5 dm^3 of blood circulating once round the body while the person is at rest, calculate the amount of oxygen transferred to the tissues.

Fig. 12. Effect of pH   *Fig. 13.* Effect of temperature   *Fig. 14.* Effect of pCO$_2$

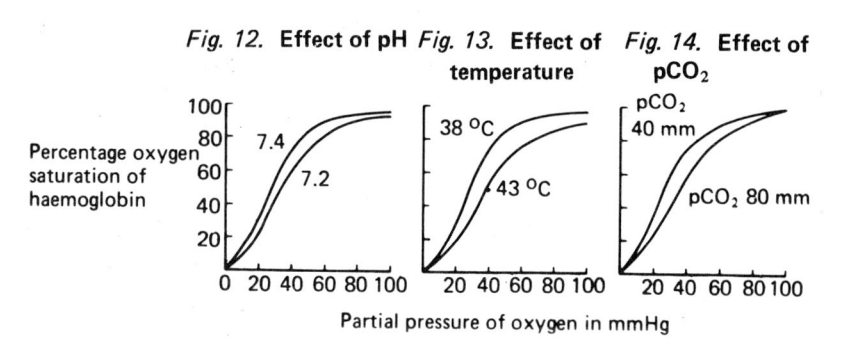

[Three graphs showing Percentage oxygen saturation of haemoglobin vs Partial pressure of oxygen in mmHg: Fig. 12 curves at pH 7.4 and 7.2; Fig. 13 curves at 38 °C and 43 °C; Fig. 14 curves at pCO$_2$ 40 mm and pCO$_2$ 80 mm]

24 Blood System

5 Fig. 15 shows the position of the dissociation curves of a foetus in relation to that of its mother. Which way will oxygen pass across the placenta, and why?

Fig. 15. **Dissociation curves of foetus and mother**

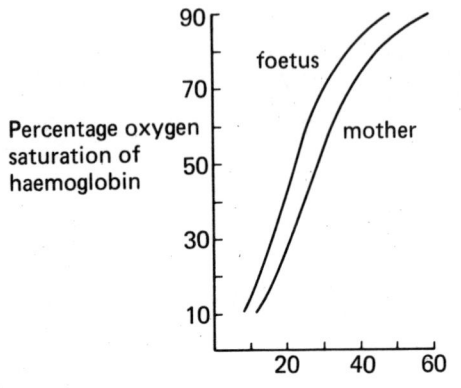

Percentage oxygen saturation of haemoglobin

Partial pressure of oxygen in mmHg

2.7 Dissociation curves

Haemoglobins of different animals can differ greatly in their oxygen affinity and in the amount of oxygen they can carry when saturated. Fig. 16 gives the dissociation curves for three animals: *Arenicola* (lugworm) which lives most of its life in a burrow in the sand just above low water mark, mackerel and man.

Fig. 16. **Oxygen haemoglobin dissociation curves for three animals**

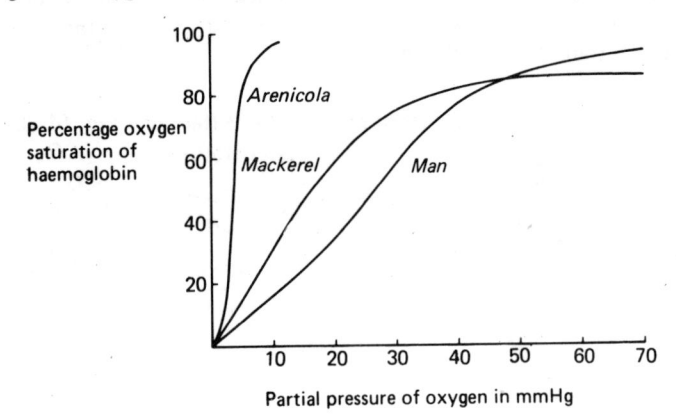

Percentage oxygen saturation of haemoglobin

Partial pressure of oxygen in mmHg

As far as you can, relate the properties of haemoglobin as shown by these graphs to the environment in which each of the three animals lives.

2.8 The transport of carbon dioxide

Carbon dioxide is carried in the blood in three ways:

a In simple solution: the solubility of carbon dioxide in blood is about twenty times that of oxygen.

b As hydrogen carbonate ions: the carbon dioxide which diffuses into red blood cells quickly reacts with water to form hydrogen carbonate ions because of the presence of the enzyme carbonic anhydrase in red blood cells.

$$CO_2 + H_2O \rightleftharpoons H^+ + HCO_3^-$$
$$\text{hydrogen carbonate ion}$$

The HCO_3^- diffuses into the plasma and the H^+ is buffered mainly by the haemoglobin.

c As carbamino compounds: some of the carbon dioxide in the plasma and red cells forms carbamino compounds with proteins, mainly haemoglobin.

These three ways are summarised in Fig. 17.

Fig. 17. Carbon dioxide in the blood. Diagram to show the volume of carbon dioxide carried in different ways

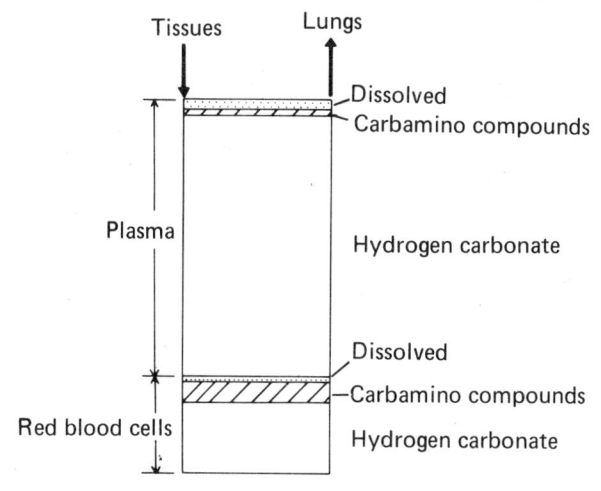

1 Is arterial or venous blood represented in the figure?
2 Which carries most carbon dioxide, the plasma or the red cells?

26 Blood System

3 In which form is **a** most **b** least carbon dioxide carried?

4 100 cm^3 of venous blood carry 55 cm^3 of carbon dioxide (with a drop in pH from 7.40 to 7.36). 100 cm^3 of arterial blood carry 50 cm^3 of carbon dioxide. What happens to the extra 5 cm^3 of carbon dioxide?

5 There are between 4.5 and 5.0 dm^3 of blood in the body, which circulate about once a minute when the body is at rest. How many cm^3 carbon dioxide are excreted per minute?

2.9 Blood groups

The existence of blood groups was not known until the beginning of this century, but blood transfusions had been attempted since the seventeenth century. Before then a blood transfusion often meant just drinking blood. The first direct transfusion was done in 1665 by Dr Lower. A small dog, nearly bled dry from a cut in the jugular vein, was kept alive by blood from two mastiffs. The connections between recipient and donors were made by quills and a piece of a large artery taken from an ox. Later, people were sometimes given blood from other species — a violent man might be given lamb's blood to make him more gentle — but in the first part of the nineteenth century it was realised that it was not safe to give man blood from other animals.

However, even transfusing human blood was not always safe. Many cases were fatal. It is to Dr Landsteiner, 1900, that we owe the explanation of the reason behind incompatible blood. He separated the cells from the plasma of different people's blood, and recombined the two in different ways. When the cells were recombined with the plasma from which they had been removed the blood appeared as normal. But when cells from one person were mixed with plasma from another the mixture would sometimes be normal, but at other times the cells would stick together in clumps (agglutinate), and the damaged red cells would break down to release haemoglobin into the plasma.

The explanation lies in different antigens and antibodies. Two different antigens, called A and B, can be present on the surface of red blood cells. The four possible blood types are given by the fact that the cells can have A antigen, B antigen, both A and B, or neither. The person's blood group is called after the antigens in the red cells, and a person with no antigens has a blood group O. The blood plasma may contain antibodies, which would react with antigens of the same type, causing agglutination, if the two met. Antibody B (called anti-B), for example, would cause agglutination with antigen B. A person's blood would not therefore contain antigens and antibodies of the same type. Plasma, however, contains antibodies of the type which do not react with antigens on the red cells. For example, if a person's red blood cells carry the A antigen only, he would carry the antibody which would react with antigen B: anti-B. If he had both A and B antigens he would have neither anti-A nor anti-B antibodies. The situation for all four blood groups is partially summarised in the table.

Blood group	O	A	B	AB
Cells: antigens	neither	A	B	A and B
Plasma: antibodies		Anti-B		neither

1 Complete the table above.
2 What will happen when
   a cells with antigen B are transferred into a recipient whose plasma contains the antibody anti-A?
   b cells with antigen B are transferred into a recipient whose plasma contains the antibody anti-B?

From the point of view of blood transfusion the important thing is that the antigens of the donor's blood should be compatible with the antibodies in the plasma of the patient receiving the transfusion: the donor's blood must not contain any antigens on the red cells which would react with the recipient's antibodies. In a small transfusion, the effect of the donor's antibodies on the recipient's red cells can be ignored as the dilution of the donor's plasma by the recipient's plasma will lower the concentration of antibodies to a level below which they do no harm.

3 Work out a chart of which transfusions will be safe, using the outlines below

a
A donor with blood group of	A	B	AB	O
can give blood to				

b
A patient with blood group of	A	B	AB	O
can be given blood from a donor of group				

28 Blood System

4 Which blood group do you think is called the

   a universal donor
   b universal recipient?

2.10 Inheritance of blood groups

Three alleles determine whether the A, B or O antigen is in a person's blood. Only two of them can be present on the pair of chromosomes which control blood group inheritance, one coming from the mother and one from the father. A child cannot therefore possess an ABO antigen which is not present in either of its parents. The ABO alleles occupy the same locus on the chromosome. If both parents contribute the same allele the child is homozygous for that characteristic and its genotype could be AA, BB or OO. If the parents contribute different alleles, the child is heterozygous and its genotype would be AB, AO or BO. A person whose genotype is AO or BO has a blood group of A or B respectively. A blood group of O appears only when the person is homozygous (OO). If both A and B are present the person has a blood group of AB.

1 Which of the three alleles

   a is the recessive
   b are the co-dominants?

2 What blood groups are possible in a child of parents with groups AB and O?

3 If parents with groups A and B produce children which show all four groups, what must have been the genotypes of the parents?

4 A paternity case is a legal case where there is a dispute as to who is the father of a child. A child in a paternity case has a blood group of O. Its mother is also O. Could the man cited in the action, whose blood group is A, be the father? Her husband's group is AB. Could he be the father?

3 Growth and Reproduction

3.1 Growth in humans

Fig. 18 shows the growth in height of an average boy from conception to age eighteen.

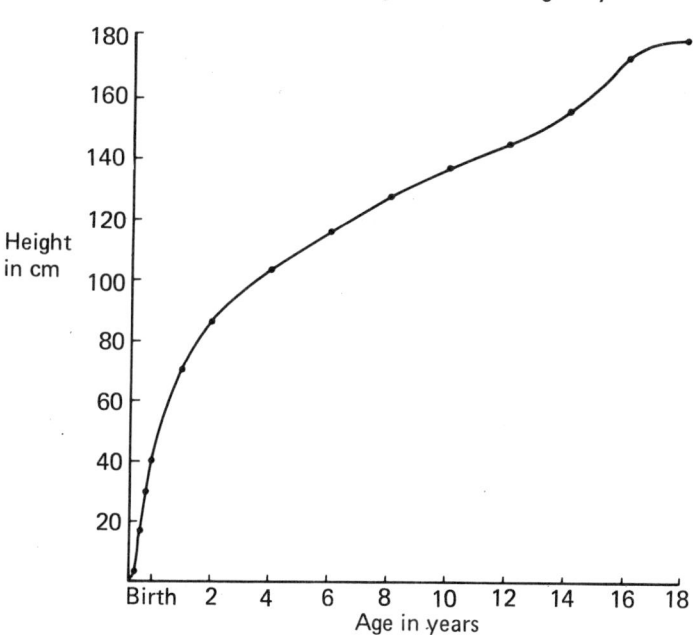

Fig. 18. **Growth in height for an average boy**

1 At what age or ages is growth quickest?
2 Which is the better criterion of growth, height or mass? Why?
3 Fig. 19 (page 30) gives the size of the head and reproductive organs, as compared with the size of the whole body at different ages. Comment on the differences between the curves.

30 Growth and Reproduction

Fig. 19. **Growth of different parts of the body**

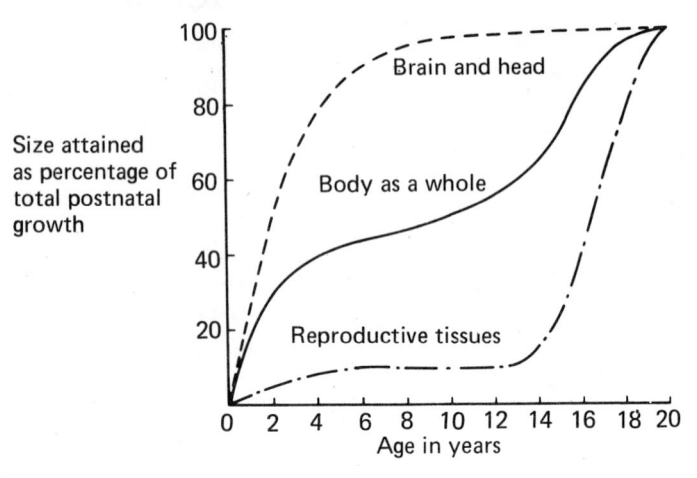

Size attained as percentage of total postnatal growth

Brain and head
Body as a whole
Reproductive tissues
Age in years

Other primates have a growth curve similar to that of man, with a peak increase in growth at or before birth, and a considerable increase again at puberty termed the adolescent spurt. Other mammals have a different growth curve. Fig. 20 gives the increase in length of a mouse over 120 days.

Fig. 20. **Growth curve for a mouse**

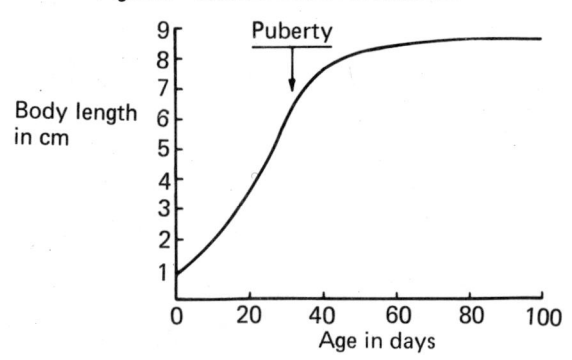

Body length in cm
Puberty
Age in days

4 Compare this curve with that for man (Fig. 18).

5 Can you see any advantage in the primate growth pattern over that of the mouse?

Figs. 21 and 22 give some of the differences in development between girls and boys.

Growth and Reproduction 31

Fig. 21. Adolescent growth spurt   *Fig. 22.* Strength of right-hand grip

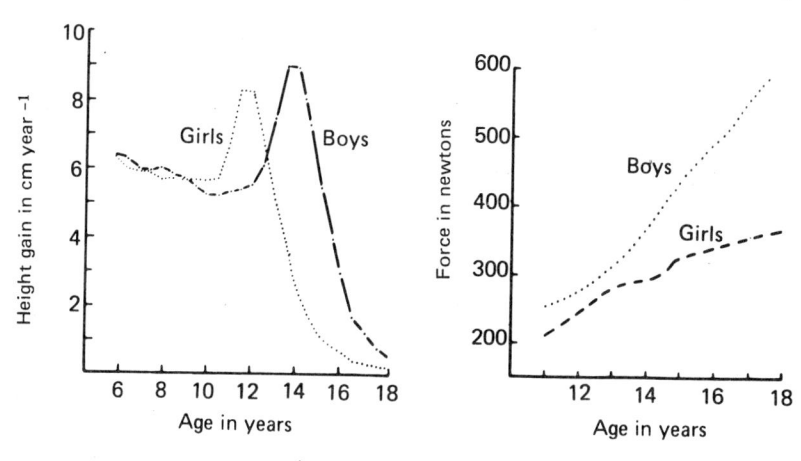

6 Relate these data to what you know of the physical differences between male and female.

3.2 Thyroid action

The thyroid hormone increases the oxygen consumption of nearly all metabolically active tissues, helps regulate lipid and carbohydrate metabolism, and is necessary for normal growth, maturation and metabolism. The function of the thyroid gland is controlled by the thyroid stimulating hormone (TSH) produced by the anterior pituitary gland. The secretion of TSH is regulated by a direct inhibitory feedback of high circulating levels of thyroid hormone on the pituitary, and also partly by neural mechanisms operating through the hypothalamus. The thyroid hormone is thyroxine, an iodine-containing amino acid.

Overactivity of the thyroid gland (hyperthyroidism) and underactivity (hypothyroidism) produce well known clinical symptoms in man. Hyperthyroidism is characterised by extreme loss of mass, trembling hands, rapid pulse, excess heat production, insensitivity to cold, nervousness, flushed face, protruding eyes and goitre. Hypothyroidism in an adult is known as myxoedema and is characterised by slow speech and movement, poor resistance to cold, a dry puffy skin and 30 to 40 per cent reduction in basal metabolic rate. In children, hypothyroidism produces a cretin with mental retardation and dwarfism.

Thyroxine acts to uncouple oxidation from phosphorylation. This means that less of the energy produced is stored in high energy phosphate bonds such as ATP and more appears as heat. It stimulates oxygen consumption and increases metabolic rate.

1 Explain as many as possible of the symptoms of hyper- and hypothyroidism in the light of the metabolic action of thyroxine.

Fig. 23 shows the action of thyroxine which was given to a person with myxoedema.

Fig. 23. **Action of thyroxine on a person with myxoedema**

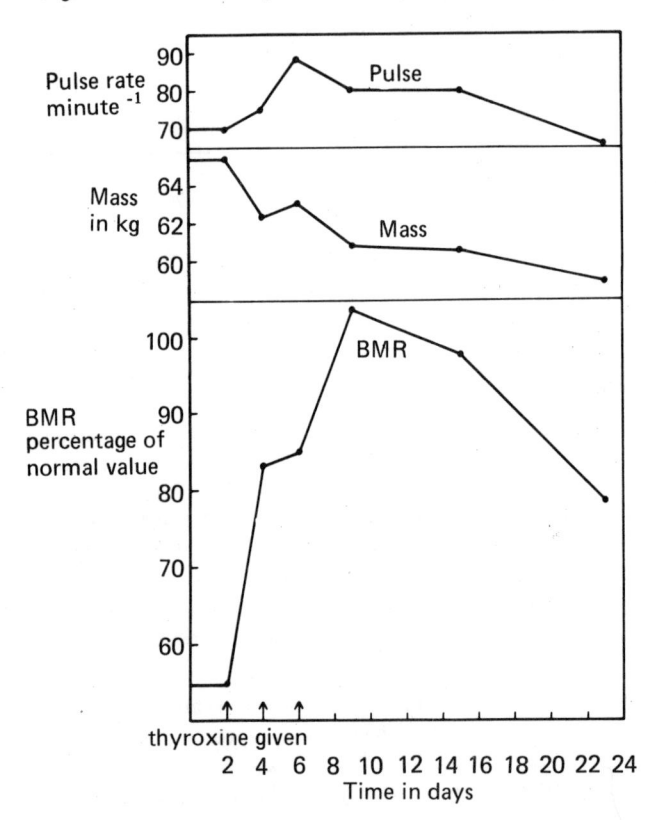

2 Explain these graphs.

Radioactive iodine (^{131}I, half life of eight days) is used to diagnose thyroid conditions. Previously thyroid activity was determined by measuring the basal metabolic rate or oxygen consumption. Now a patient can drink a liquid containing radioactive iodine. The rate of uptake of the iodine, the amount taken up and its release from the gland is found out. The difference between the activity of normal and abnormal glands can be detected by measuring the amount of radioactivity in the gland or the urine.

Fig. 24 shows uptake of radioactive iodine by the thyroid and its excretion in a normal person, and in people suffering from hyper- or hypothyroidism.

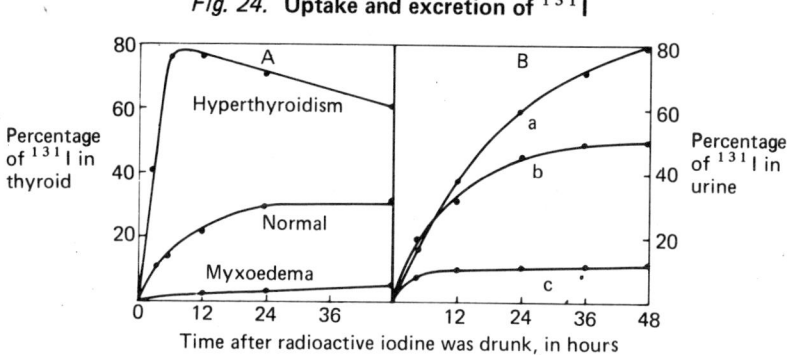

Fig. 24. Uptake and excretion of ^{131}I

3 Label the curves on graph B.

4 How do these results relate to the over- and underactivity of the thyroid gland and enable a diagnosis of thyroid activity to be made?

3.3 Nature and nurture

There has been a great deal of discussion this century, and particularly in recent years, on the relative importance of inheritance and environment on the intellectual development and attainment of children (the Nature-Nurture controversy). From the end of the nineteenth century to the mid 1940s the importance of heredity was stressed. It was widely believed that a person was born with a fixed, innate intelligence which rarely varied very much during his or her life. This 'fixed intelligence' was an inborn personal ability and it justified the idea of a constant intelligence quotient (I.Q.). Any one measurement of I.Q. could predict a person's development and all his future I.Q. measurements. The I.Q. and rate of development was predetermined and fixed, once and for all, by a person's genotype. Sir Cyril Burt wrote in 1934 that by intelligence, the psychologist understood inborn, all-round intellectual ability. It was inherited, or at least innate, not due to teaching or training, and it remained uninfluenced by industry or zeal.

There were, however, some people who held the opposite view. Even as early as 1909, Alfred Binet, a French educationist, opposed this 'brutal

34 Growth and Reproduction

pessimism' and said that a child's mind was like a field for which a farmer had advised a change in the method of cultivating, with the result that in place of desert land, we now had a harvest. In this sense he maintained that the intelligence of children could be increased.

The implications of the belief in a fixed and totally inherited intelligence were far reaching: it influenced the development, education and welfare of children. Among other things, the blame for failure was removed from the home, school, teacher or the educational system, and placed squarely on the child's shoulders. A sow's ear would remain as such and no amount of effort in the classroom would convert it into anything approaching a silk purse. In child-rearing a baby had only to grow, in an automatic way, for any potentiality to blossom. Mothers were warned (especially 1915-35) not to play with a young child in case he got too much stimulation which might interfere with his growth, and not to spoil him with a lot of fussy loving. Because intelligence and other characteristics were fixed, it was important to get round pegs in round holes – leading to overemphasis on selection, and underemphasis on training.

Charles Darwin's *The Origin of Species* in 1859 provided evidence to support the view that inherited variations were passed on, and his views replaced those of Lamarck who had written much about acquired characteristics. Francis Galton, Darwin's cousin, in his book *Hereditary Genius*, 1869, also supplied evidence for those who believed in heredity. As part of his argument he discussed his own family, showing to his mind that scientific distinction was clearly inherited.

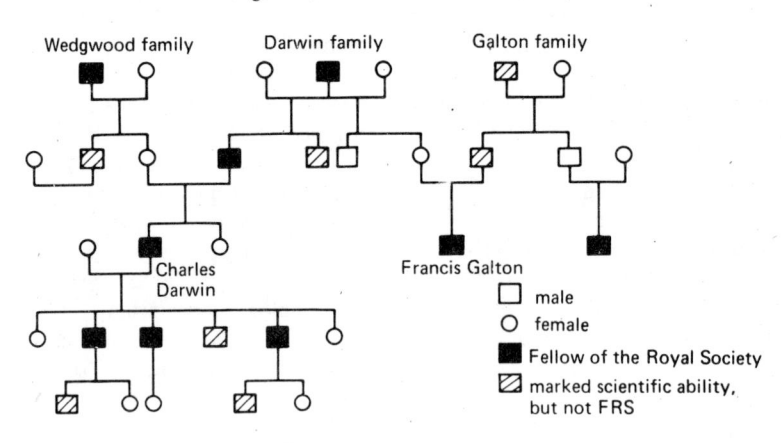

Fig. 25. **Some of Galton's family**

1. There are serious flaws in Galton's piece of evidence. Point them out.

2 Do you think there are anatomical and biochemical features to which intelligence could be related? If so, what?

One of the sources of evidence for both environmentalists and those who believe in the importance of inheritance has come from studying correlations between related and unrelated groups of people. (Correlations are noted on a scale ranging from -1 to +1. If two groups have a correlation of +1 then they are similar. A correlation of 0 means that they are totally unrelated, and a correlation of -1 means one is the opposite of the other. Figures of 0.7 and above indicate a high degree of correlation). If, therefore, intelligence were caused entirely by inheritance, one would expect two people of exactly similar inheritance (identical twins) to have a correlation of +1. There would be a 100 per cent chance of successfully predicting one's characteristics from the other. One would also expect no correlation (0) between totally unrelated groups of people, even those brought up in the same house.

Correlations for intellectual ability

Correlations between	Obtained median value	Theoretical value
Unrelated persons		
Children reared apart	−0.01	0
Foster parent and child	+0.20	0
Children reared together	+0.24	0
Related persons		
Second cousins	+0.16	+0.063
First cousins	+0.26	+0.125
Siblings, reared apart	+0.47	+0.50
Siblings, reared together	+0.55	+0.50
Non-identical twins, different sex	+0.49	+0.50
Non-identical twins, same sex	+0.56	+0.50
Identical twins, reared apart	+0.75	+1.0
Identical twins, reared together	+0.87	+1.0
Parent and child	+0.50	+0.50

A large number of studies have been done of the measured I.Q. of a lot of people; unrelated people and identical twins, children reared apart and together, foster children and parents, and so on. A number of these studies were collected together and summarised by A.R. Jensen to produce the table above. The actual correlations between people are given as an average of all the studies considered, together with the correlation one would expect

36 Growth and Reproduction

if intellectual ability were entirely due to inheritance, assuming the simplest possible polygenic model.

3 Analyse the extent to which these data support the view of a fixed, inherited intelligence.

Some twin studies have included data on physical characteristics, such as the height and mass of twins. The next table gives correlation data for female twins from one such study. (Not all studies were strictly comparable.)

Correlations for female twins

| | Identical twins || Non-identical twins reared together |
	reared together	reared apart	
Height	+0.94	+0.82	+0.44
Mass	+0.81	+0.37	+0.56

4 To what extent do these correlations support
  a the inheritance view
  b the environmentalist view?

One might think that studies of identical and non-identical twins reared apart and together would go a long way towards settling the nature-nurture controversy: each of the two variables could be kept constant in turn, children of identical heredity in two different environments, and children of different heredity in the same environment. But it isn't as easy as this. For a start, the influence of the internal prenatal environment cannot be analysed: there may have been differences in nutrition and so on before birth which the investigator would never know about. Even twins reared apart are perhaps not in widely dissimilar environments. They probably live in the same kind of house and neighbourhood, and most certainly in the same culture. In fact, the studies on twins provide examples of close similarity in spite of different environments, differences probably due to environment, and differences difficult to interpret.

One of the pairs of separated twins much quoted is Gladys and Helen. They were separated at the age of eighteen months and met again when they were twenty-eight. At age thirty-five there was a test score difference between them of twenty-four points. Helen had the higher score. She had stayed with her family, had a university education and taught for twelve years. She had social polish and charm. Gladys had been adopted by a railway conductor who had retired and moved because of ill health when Gladys had done only three years at school. After that she didn't go to school again but worked in a mill and shops.

Growth and Reproduction 37

5 Suggest reasons why Gladys's score could have been so much lower than her sister's.

Other evidence for the controversy has come from many sources including studies of adopted and orphanage children, gifted children, people with brain damage, and children from very deprived environments. Two early studies (1923) on deprived environments considered canal boat children and gipsy children. The canal boat children spent only five per cent of the school year at school, living for most of the time on the boats. Their measured intelligence declined with age. At four to six years the average test score gave an I.Q. of 90, by twelve to twenty-two it had dropped to 60. The age:IQ correlation was -0.755. The gipsy children were at school for 35 per cent of the school year, and when at home they were not isolated in a boat on water. Their I.Q. dropped with age too, not to such a great extent, but there was still a negative correlation of -0.430 between age and I.Q.

6 Discuss reasons for the negative correlation between age and intelligence score in these two groups.

In recent years a very great deal of work has been done. Evidence is gathering to contradict the view held in the early part of the century that intelligence is governed only by heredity, and there is now massive support for the view that the environment can enhance or modify inherited ability to a certain and unknown extent. Intelligence and attainment scores have been gathered for many thousands of children and students. There are large numbers of tables and graphs. Very briefly, some of the results from all this work are summarised below. Because the general trends are drawn from so many studies and such very large numbers there will of course be many individual exceptions to trends noted.

a Family size. Average test scores show a steady drop with increasing number of children in a family. On average, children from large families do not do as well as children from small families.

b Sibling position. First-born children seem to do better than those born later. Average test scores show that only children do slightly better than eldest children of other families, who in their turn do better than their younger siblings. In a family of more than two, the next best performer is often the youngest, then the intermediates. There are differences here between boys and girls: for example, eldest children who are boys tend to do better than those who are girls.

c Social class. In every occupational category of parents (higher professional, managerial and other professional, highly skilled, clerical, semi-skilled, unskilled, casual) the test scores of children range from the highest possible to the lowest. There is a very wide spread of ability in each category and therefore considerable overlap between categories. But as one goes from the unskilled to the higher professional category average test scores of the children rise steadily.

d **Parental education and encouragement.** Again on average, children who have parents with a high level of interest in them and their progress, or whose parents are well educated themselves, tend to do better at school than those with uninterested or uneducated parents.

e **Home and School.** Children who are better housed, who attend a primary school which has a good record, whose own attitude to school is a positive one, who work hard, who show few or no symptoms of disturbed behaviour, who do not play truant, who are put into a top stream, tend to do better than children at the other end of the scale.

7 Discuss possible reasons for the trends a to e listed above.

In summary, it seems obvious that inheritance must influence intelligence. Intelligence is a property of a brain, which is made up of cells that depend on enzyme systems for their working. Presumably the genes operate to prescribe the direction of development, and set irrevocable limits on the range of capacities which can be developed. Not everyone is capable of becoming an Einstein no matter how favourable their upbringing and environment. And other people win through to the highest distinction despite many unfavourable conditions. What we don't know, of course, is whether they would have done even better without the difficulties they overcame. Does the genotype provide controlling directives for development and set limits for the range of phenotypic variation? Do the encounters a child has with his or her environment as he or she develops react on the genotype to determine to a certain extent further development? Does a child respond to the circumstances encountered with the structures already developed, which perhaps develop further as they adapt to a changing environment? Does therefore the phenotypic intelligence of a child depend on his genotype and the succession of circumstances he encounters?

Not enough is yet known about the subject to give a percentage to each influence. Indeed the variables are so many, and so little known, it may never be possible to do so with any certainty. It may even be that the percentage varies with each individual, which makes the task even more formidable. We do know, however, that hereditary traits can be modified. Some hereditary diseases, once thought to be inevitable or uncurable, can respond to diet, exercises, education, drugs. On the other hand, there is a belief that differences caused by the environment are unreal or temporary. Again this is not true. Prejudices are difficult to erase, low stature caused by poor feeding in childhood cannot be changed. Perhaps hereditary intelligence responds in a similar way.

3.4 Control of menstrual cycle

The menstrual cycle in women is controlled by hormones produced by the pituitary gland and the ovary. Fig. 26 gives a summary of the hormones

Growth and Reproduction 39

and their effects. This picture has been built up by experiments on rats and other animals, and from medical observations on women.

Fig. 26. **Control of menstrual cycle**

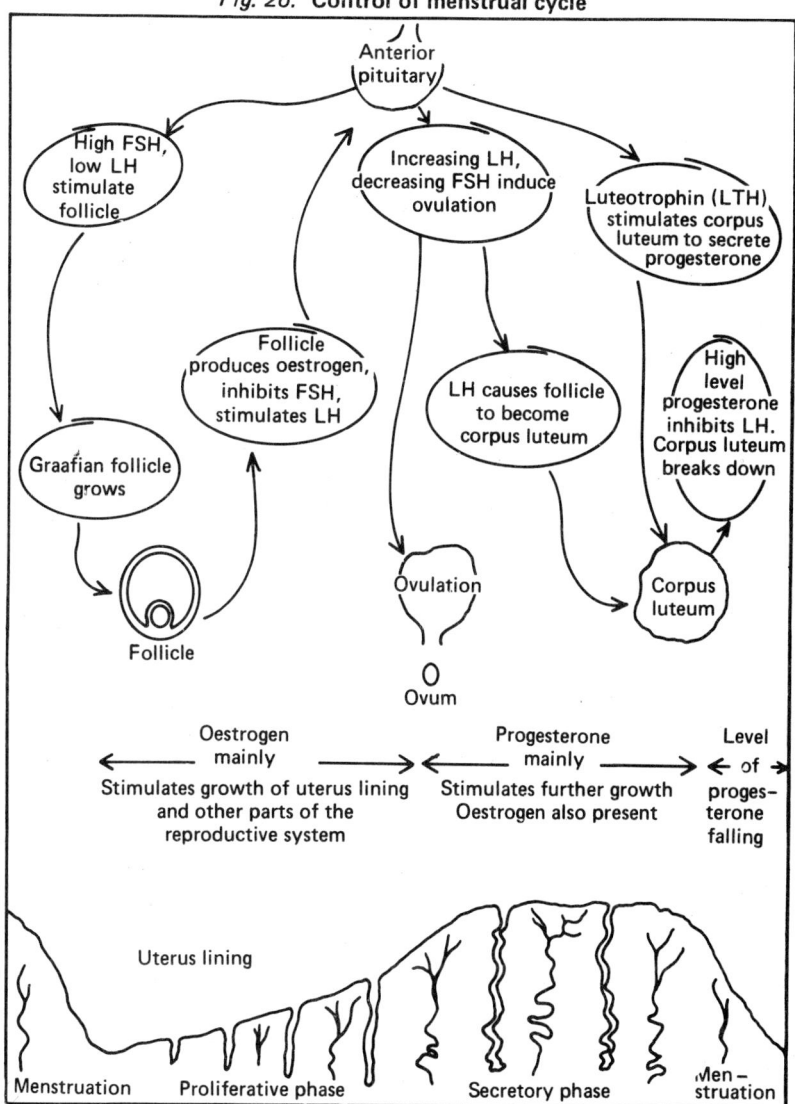

Anterior pituitary

High FSH, low LH stimulate follicle

Increasing LH, decreasing FSH induce ovulation

Luteotrophin (LTH) stimulates corpus luteum to secrete progesterone

Follicle produces oestrogen, inhibits FSH, stimulates LH

LH causes follicle to become corpus luteum

High level progesterone inhibits LH. Corpus luteum breaks down

Graafian follicle grows

Follicle

Ovulation

O
Ovum

Corpus luteum

⟵ Oestrogen mainly ⟶ ⟵ Progesterone mainly ⟶ ⟵ Level of proges- terone falling ⟶

Stimulates growth of uterus lining and other parts of the reproductive system

Stimulates further growth Oestrogen also present

Uterus lining

Menstruation | Proliferative phase | Secretory phase | Men- struation

Two lists follow. The first one, numbers **1** to **5**, gives some of the observations. The second list, **A** to **G**, gives some of the conclusions drawn from the work done in the field. Say which of the observations **1** to **5**

40 Growth and Reproduction

support each of the conclusions. Some observations support more than one conclusion.

Observations

1. a If the pituitary gland is removed from an immature mammal the gonads do not mature and secondary sexual characteristics do not appear
   b If the pituitary is removed from an adult the ovaries and uterus stop working.
   c A suspension of the anterior pituitary injected into adult females whose ovaries are intact is followed by immediate maturation of ova; injection into an immature female with intact ovaries is followed by oestrus. Injection into an animal with no ovaries gives no results.
   d Injection of some relatively purified pituitary extracts produces growth mainly of the ovarian follicles, others induce ovulation and the formation of corpora lutea as well.

2. a If the ovaries are removed (leaving the pituitary and uterus intact) from an immature female, the uterus never starts functioning.
   b If the ovaries are removed from mature women the menstrual cycle stops, the vagina and uterus atrophy, and the endometrium (uterus lining) becomes very thin.

3. The ovaries produce two types of hormone, oestrogen and progesterone. If the ovaries are removed, treatment with oestrogens restores the vagina (2b) to normal, and brings the uterus to the stage characteristic of the middle of a normal menstrual cycle. If now progesterone as well as oestrogen is injected, the uterus progresses as normal towards menstruation. Stopping the hormones causes bleeding as in menstruation.

4. The injection of one of the pituitary hormones, follicle-stimulating hormone (FSH), into animals whose pituitary has been removed causes only slight growth of the ovarian follicles, with only a small output of oestrogen from the ovaries. The injection of luteinising hormone (LH), also produced by the pituitary, into animals with no pituitary, increases the amount of oestrogen but doesn't stimulate the follicles. FSH and LH injected together cause the normal cycle: growth of a follicle, oestrogen output, and ovulation.

5. If the ovaries are removed, or after the menopause when they have ceased to function, there is an increased amount of FSH in the body.

Conclusions

A The pituitary influences the development and function of the ovaries and uterus.
B The pituitary has no direct effect on the cycle but exerts its effect through an inductive action on the ovary.
C The ovarian hormones are responsible for the changes in the vagina and

Growth and Reproduction   41

uterus in the menstrual cycle.

D Both ovarian hormones are needed for a complete menstrual cycle, although oestrogen alone will initiate it.

E Two pituitary hormones work together to produce the normal cycle in the ovary.

F Something produced by the ovary inhibits the production of FSH by the pituitary.

G A simplified version of control of the menstrual cycle is: The pituitary produces hormones which stimulate the ovary to produce its hormones. These stimulate the uterus to activity. The ovarian hormones reach a level high enough to inhibit the pituitary, which then stops stimulating the ovary. The ovary stops producing its hormone and the uterus reverts to its original state. When inhibition of the pituitary ceases, the cycle starts again. This is a negative feedback mechanism.

3.5 Ovulation and temperature

In an overpopulated world it may seem strange that infertility should be a problem. Yet for some couples the inability to have a child can be a source of sorrow or self-reproach and they may approach a doctor to discover the cause. A woman who seeks advice after having tried unsuccessfully to conceive will probably first be asked to keep a record of her daily temperature.

The normal temperature of a healthy person is 37 °C although there are usually slight variations around this figure. However, for a woman between the ages of about thirteen and forty-five the temperature picture is complicated by the menstrual cycle. Ovulation occurs only once during each cycle and the time of ovulation can often be determined by recording body temperature which is lower during the first part of the menstrual cycle than during the second. It is only after ovulation that it climbs to the 'normal' of 37 °C. It starts to fall again just before the next period is due. The temperature is taken once a day, usually in the morning before getting up, and recorded on a graph. Ovulation is indicated by a rise of 0.2 to 0.35 °C above the previous level, particularly if the rise occurs in the middle of the cycle (about fourteen days before the next period is expected on a twenty-eight day cycle) and if it corresponds with a similar rise in graphs of previous cycles. Often, too, the temperature drops 0.1 to 0.2 °C the day before it rises. For women wishing to become pregnant, or to avoid pregnancy, it is of course important to know the time of ovulation as precisely as possible. Intercourse during the twenty-four hours following the temperature drop or during the twenty-four hours after the temperature rise gives the best chance of conception.

The egg lives for about twelve to possibly twenty-four hours after ovulation as it travels down the Fallopian tube. Sperms deposited during

42 Growth and Reproduction

intercourse can live for about forty-eight hours within the female reproductive system. These times vary slightly in different books and no doubt in different women. A couple wanting a child should therefore have intercourse during the two days around ovulation. A couple not wanting to conceive should be more careful and leave a longer gap around the time of ovulation, or preferably rely on a more efficient means of contraception than use of the 'safe period'.

Fig. 27 is a hypothetical, average graph drawn to illustrate these points for a woman with a twenty-eight day cycle. The first day of the period is called Day 1.

Fig. 27. **Temperature during one twenty-eight day cycle**

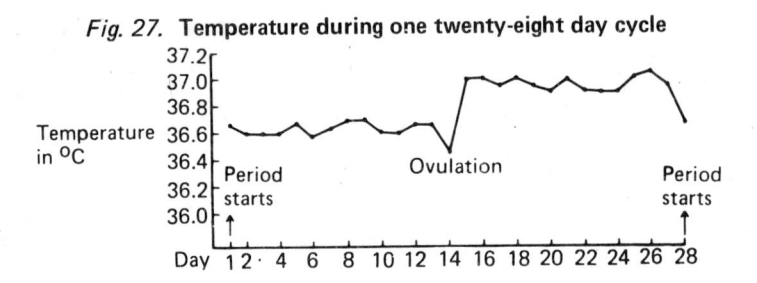

Few women, however, can produce a good typical graph or for that matter regular twenty-eight day cycles. More likely the monthly cycle varies unpredictably in length, and the temperature pattern could be disturbed by a cold or distress, or the rise to normal after ovulation could take several days.

Fig. 28 gives the actual temperatures for two consecutive months for a woman whose cycle varied from twenty-one to twenty-nine days. During the second one she conceived.

Fig. 28. **Temperature during two cycles**

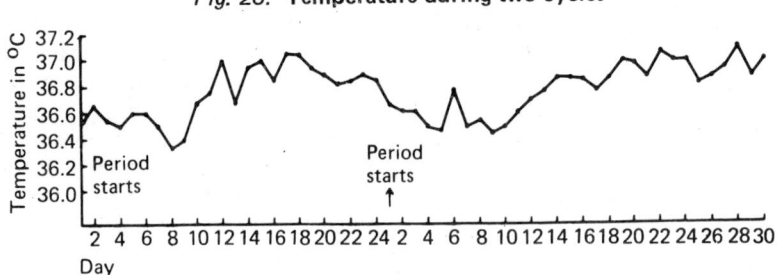

1 Interpret these graphs as far as you can. Say where you think conception occurred.

Growth and Reproduction 43

One way of birth control, and the only one allowed by the Roman Catholic church, is to use the 'safe period'. But because the sperms can live for up to two days in the uterus, because of the variability in the length of many women's cycles, and because the egg can be released on any one of about five days in the middle of the month, a woman may not know whether she was still in the safe period or not until two weeks afterwards, when it is either all right or too late. Books on contraception give advice on how to calculate unsafe times.

2 Work out the possible unsafe times for a woman with a regular twenty-eight day cycle, wishing to avoid a pregnancy. Do the same for the woman in question 1 whose cycle ranged from twenty-one to twenty-nine days.

3.6 Gametogenesis

The diagram summarises the process of gametogenesis in mammals, resulting in the formation of ova and spermatozoa. The twenty-third pair of chromosomes is the sex pair, XX in a female, XY in a male.

Fig. 29. **Gametogenesis**

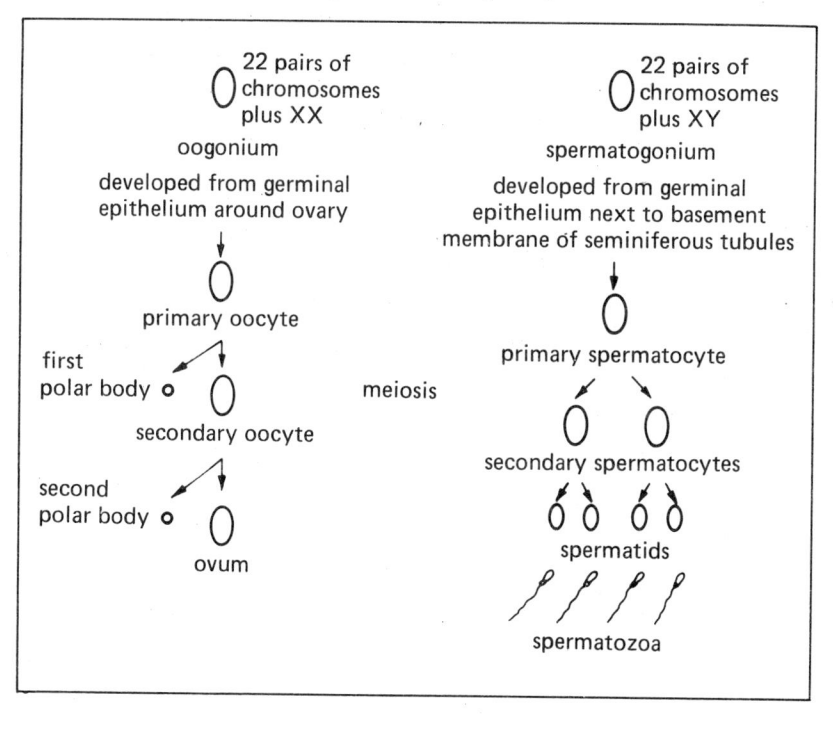

```
            22 pairs of                        22 pairs of
         O  chromosomes                     O  chromosomes
            plus XX                            plus XY
            oogonium                           spermatogonium
      developed from germinal           developed from germinal
      epithelium around ovary           epithelium next to basement
                                        membrane of seminiferous tubules
                 ↓                                   ↓
                 O                                   O
            primary oocyte                      primary spermatocyte
  first        ↗ ↑                                  ↙  ↘
  polar body o   O          meiosis              O     O
            secondary oocyte                secondary spermatocytes
  second       ↗ ↑                             ↙ ↘   ↙ ↘
  polar body o   O                            O  O   O  O
                ovum                             spermatids
                                                 ♂ ♂ ♂ ♂
                                                spermatozoa
```

44 Growth and Reproduction

1 Compare the processes of oogenesis and spermatogenesis.
2 Which parent determines whether the offspring is to be male or female, and how?
3 Egg cells are much larger than sperms. Comment on the differences in size.
4 What is the function of fertilisation?

3.7 Artificial insemination

There was a local superstition in a part of Africa that a cow inseminated in the evening with a small amount of fresh diluted bull semen would produce a female calf, while one inseminated with semen from the same sample twelve hours later during the next morning would produce a male. Consequently farmers were demanding that their cows be inseminated in the evening instead of the more usual first part of the day. Usually the bull semen was collected in the afternoon, diluted with an egg yolk mixture, and stored in tubes at 4 °C until a little was taken from a tube and used to inseminate a cow. On investigating all the records it was discovered that there seemed to be some basis for the superstition, in that instead of the expected roughly equal proportions of male and female calves, 60 per cent of the calves produced from morning inseminations were male.

In looking for an explanation for this phenomenon, factors concerned with the collection and storage of the sperm were first investigated.

1 What factors could have been examined in this initial investigation?

The next investigation involved taking a closer look at the sperm in the tube. It was seen that sperm and dilutant had been adequately mixed and that the sperms were still viable. Counts of sperms were then made at thirteen levels down the tube after it had been standing for some hours. Results gave the graph below.

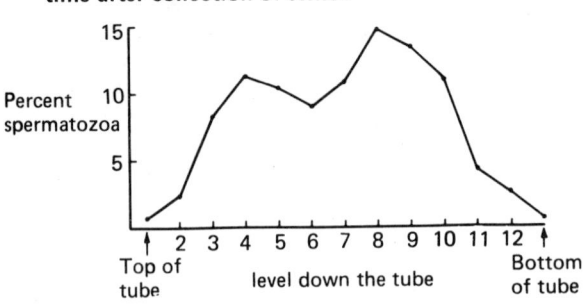

Fig. 30. **Sperm counts at various levels in a tube some time after collection of semen**

2 Suggest a possible reason to explain the shape of this curve.
3 How could you continue the investigation to try and confirm your hypothesis?
4 Why do you think the morning-inseminated cows produced more male calves than female?
5 Bird semen, treated in a similar way, gives only one peak. Why?

3.8 Reproductive behaviour

The table gives information relating to reproductive behaviour and development of a number of animals.

Species	No. of eggs or young produced at any one time	Mates in water or on land	If a mating position is adopted	Develops in water, shelled egg, or mother	Length of parental care after birth
Cod	3–7 million	W	X	W	–
Frog	1000-2000	W	√	W	–
Adder	10–14	L	√	E	–
Partridge	8–16	L	√	E	about 3 weeks
Blackbird	3–6	L	√	E	about 3 weeks
Cat	4	L	√	M	about 4 weeks
Man	1	L	√	M	18 years or longer

1 Say, with reasons, which of the eggs is likely to have
   a the most yolk
   b the least yolk.
2 Compare the number of eggs produced by the fish with the number produced by the frog. Suggest one reason from the data given which might go some way towards explaining the difference.
3 Suggest a hypothesis, based on the nesting behaviour of the partridge and the blackbird, which might be put forward to account in part for the difference in the number of eggs they lay.
4 Of those outlined in the table which way of reproduction do you think is the most efficient and why?
5 In a stable population what relationship would you expect to find between the total number of individuals in a species and the number of offspring which reach sexual maturity?

46 Growth and Reproduction

3.9 Hatching and temperature

The table gives the number of hours from laying to hatching of the eggs of *Xenopus laevis* at four temperatures.

Temperature in °C	Hours to hatching
15	165
22	39
25	34
30	28

1 What relationship, if any, can you see between temperature and time to hatching? Explain any relationship you find.

A similar table showing the relationship between hatching time and temperature for trout found in British waters is given below.

Temperature in °C	Days to hatching
5	82
10	41
15	27
22	die
25	die
30	die

2 Comment on the difference between the two species with regard to the length of time to hatching.

3.10 Growth-controlling products in tadpoles

Tadpoles begin to grow at different rates after hatching. When rearing a number of frog tadpoles in about a litre of water it is often noted that tadpoles which grow most rapidly at first continue to grow. Those which grow slowly at first stop growing and die if left in the aquarium, but they can grow rapidly if removed and reared singly.

One hypothesis put forward to explain this effect was that the larger tadpoles were excreting into the water growth-controlling products which

inhibited the growth of the smaller tadpoles.
1 Suggest two other hypotheses which might explain the slow growth and death of some tadpoles.
2 What experiments would you set up to test your two hypotheses?
3 In fact it was discovered that the production of a growth-controlling compound was the correct explanation. How would you set up an experiment to see if this was true?

3.11 Metamorphosis in frogs

The mechanism of control of metamorphosis in amphibians has been the object of much research for many years. In 1912 the German biologist Friedrich Gudernatsch made the first discovery given in the list of evidence which follows. Since then more and more research work has led to the accumulation of evidence leading to conclusions about the mechanism involved.

Below are given a number of pieces of evidence (**1** to **12**) and the conclusions which were drawn from them (**A** to **I**). Say which pieces of evidence you think contributed to each of the conclusions listed.

Evidence

1 Feeding tadpoles with an extract from the thyroid gland caused, within a week, the typical signs of metamorphosis: rapid growth of legs, widening of the mouth, resorption of the tail.

2 Feeding the thyroid hormone thyroxine to tadpoles had the same effect as a thyroid extract.

3 In tadpoles which had not started to metamorphose the thyroid is small and its cells appear inactive. During the early part of metamorphosis (when the hind legs start to grow) the thyroid grows rapidly. At the climax (when the fore legs emerge) it is large and very active.

4 Tadpoles which had their thyroid glands removed did not metamorphose.

5 Giving thyrectomised tadpoles a low dose of thyroxine throughout metamorphosis caused normal metamorphosis in the early stages, but very slow later stages. Giving a low dose at first, and then increasing it about twenty times later on, caused metamorphosis to proceed at its normal speed and timing.

6 Tadpoles with pituitary glands removed did not metamorphose.

7 Tadpoles which had their pituitary gland removed from the undersurface of the brain and transplanted to another part of the body at an early stage did not metamorphose normally. Most eventually showed some leg growth but their progress was very much slower than normal, and some showed no

Growth and Reproduction

metamorphic changes at all. None proceeded further than the start of the climax phase.

8 If, instead of removing the pituitary, the part of the hypothalamus in the brain to which it is attached was removed, metamorphosis proceeded through the early stages but stopped abruptly when it reached the climax stage. The pituitary did not degenerate when it was cut off in this way and was functional with regard to other hormones it produced.

9 If a barrier was placed between the brain and the pituitary, the same results as in **8** were noted.

10 Some nerve cells manufacture hormone-like substances (neurosecretions) which travel along the nerve-cell fibres and are released at their ends. The hypothalamus is connected to the pituitary by a special set of 'portal veins' which receive blood from a net of capillaries inside a structure called the median eminence. This sends blood directly to the pituitary, not to the heart. Nerve fibres carrying neurosecretions terminate in the median eminence. When the animal had regenerated the portal blood vessels which by-passed the barrier interposed between the brain and pituitary (**9**), metamorphosis proceeded normally.

11 Young tadpoles lack a fully developed median eminence. It develops at the early stage of metamorphosis. Removing the early tadpole's thyroid also prevented development of the median eminence. Giving thyroxine to such a tadpole allowed the median eminence to develop.

12 Giving thyroxine to very young tadpoles did not start a precocious development of metamorphosis, or affect the median eminence. The median eminence of tadpoles at various later stages of development showed an increasing sensitivity to thyroxine.

Conclusions

A The thyroid hormone plays a critical part in producing tadpole metamorphosis.

B The progress of metamorphosis is connected with increasing activity of the thyroid.

C The thyroid's activity is controlled by the pituitary gland (in fact by a thyroid stimulating hormone, TSH).

D The stimulus which starts the pituitary production of TSH does not come from another endocrine gland.

E Metamorphic failure on disconnecting the pituitary is not due to its degeneration, but to lack of connection between the pituitary and brain.

F Early metamorphosis, requiring only a low level of hormone, can proceed without direct stimulation from the brain.

G There exists a mechanism by which the hypothalamus can send chemical

Growth and Reproduction 49

stimuli direct to the pituitary, and the hypothalamus therefore regulates metamorphosis, not through nerves, but through chemical messages passing by way of the portal veins to the pituitary.

H   A positive feedback mechanism operates in the tadpole: thyroxine causes the median eminence to develop which stimulates the pituitary to activate the thyroid to produce more hormone.

A positive feedback system of this sort will lead to an intense build-up of activity. This is what is noted in metamorphosis. From low activity at the start it builds up to a very high activity at the climax.

I   Thyroxine triggers the metamorphic mechanism only after the tadpole has reached a certain age of maturity.

There is also evidence to show that thyroxine acts directly on the pituitary to inhibit its production of TSH. This negative feedback system keeps the levels of thyroxine and TSH in balance with each other at a level which is determined by the sensitivity of the pituitary to thyroid inhibition.

3.12 Litter size and survival

Pig litters range in size from about three to eighteen piglets per litter.

The average number of piglets surviving in litters was determined three and six weeks after birth. Fig. 31 gives the results of the investigation.

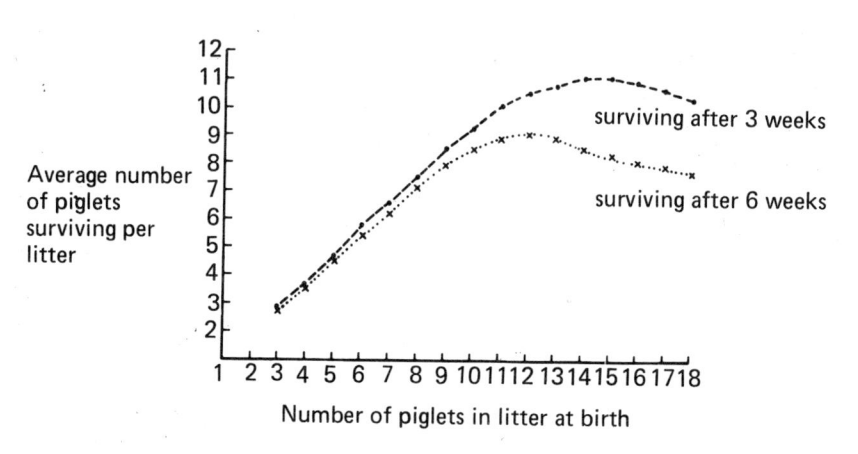

Fig. 31. Litter size and survival in pigs

1 What, from the data, seems to be the optimum litter size for maximum survival?

50 Growth and Reproduction

2 Comment on the results.
3 How would you expect the results to differ in wild pigs?
4 What average number of offspring would you expect to survive to maturity from a pair of wild pigs?

4 Excretion

4.1 Urea production and excretion

The graphs in Fig. 32 show the effect of the removal of liver and kidneys in dogs on the amount of urea in the blood. On the graphs the time when the liver was removed is marked by a cross and the time when the kidneys were removed by a circle. All the graphs have a similar starting point, the normal level of blood urea for the animal.

Fig. 32. **Blood urea nitrogen after removal of liver and/or kidneys**

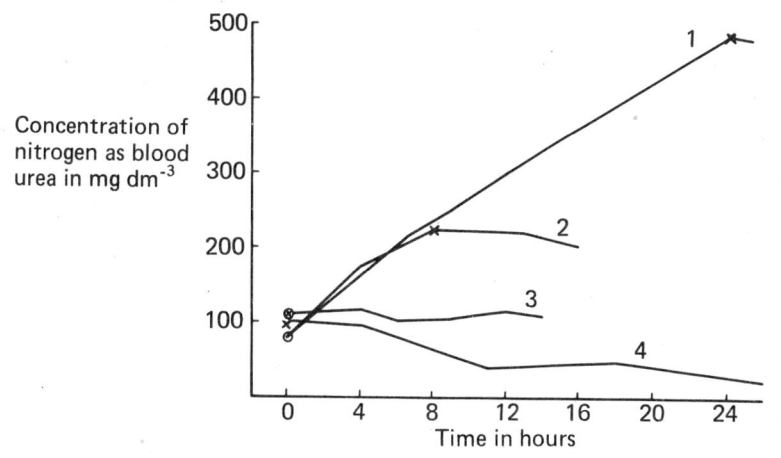

[Graph: x-axis "Time in hours" from 0 to 24; y-axis "Concentration of nitrogen as blood urea in mg dm^{-3}" from 0 to 500. Four curves labelled 1, 2, 3, 4.]

1 Kidneys removed at Time 0, liver twenty-four hours later.
2 Kidneys removed at Time 0, liver eight hours later.
3 Kidneys and liver removed at Time 0.
4 Liver removed at Time 0, kidneys not removed.

Interpret these graphs in terms of the functions of the kidneys and liver.

4.2 Nitrogenous excretion in man

The table (page 52) gives the concentration of a number of substances in the plasma and urine of man.

52 Excretion

	Plasma concentration in g dm^{-3}	Urine concentration in g dm^{-3}
Water	900 to 930	950
Proteins and other colloids	70 to 80	0
Glucose	1.0	0
Urea	0.3	20
Uric acid	0.03	20
Creatinine	0.01	1.0
Ammonia	0.001	0.5
Sodium	3.2	6.0
Potassium	0.2	1.5
Calcium	0.1	0.15
Magnesium	0.025	0.1
Chloride, as Cl	3.7	6.0
Phosphate, inorganic, as P	0.03	1.2
Sulphate, as H$_2$SO$_4$	0.03	1.8

1 From the table list those substances which are excreted by the kidney.
2 Which substances are not excreted at all?
3 Urea, uric acid, creatinine and ammonia contain nitrogen and are produced by the body either from excess protein eaten or from body tissue protein broken down. Of these four substances only the amount of creatinine excreted remains approximately the same when excretion on a protein rich diet is compared with excretion on a protein poor diet. The excretion of the other three rises sharply as the amount of protein in the diet is increased. What does this suggest about the source of the creatinine as compared with the source of the other excretory products?
4 The pH of the plasma varies between narrow limits 7.35 − 7.45. The pH of the urine varies between 4.5 and 8 (usually about 6). Apart from controlling the water balance of the body and excreting nitrogenous waste, what other function do you think the kidney has?

4.3 Nitrogenous excretion in vertebrates

Three main nitrogenous excretory substances are produced by different vertebrates:

a Ammonia, a highly toxic substance which must be disposed of rapidly. It diffuses quickly from the animal if there is plenty of water. If it cannot

Excretion 53

be rapidly excreted it has to be converted to some other, less toxic, substance.
b Urea, which is non-toxic even in quite high concentrations and can therefore be retained in the body for some time before it is excreted. It is very soluble and diffusible.
c Uric acid, which is non-toxic. It is relatively insoluble and can be precipitated as a solid in a crystalline form for storage and later excretion. As it is insoluble it exerts no osmotic effect when in its crystalline form.

Ammonia is the primary product of excretion and is produced during the deamination of amino acids during nitrogen metabolism in vertebrates. Urea and uric acid are synthesised from ammonia. The synthesis is complex and involves the expenditure of energy.

The table below gives details of the main end-products of nitrogenous excretion in vertebrates, together with details of habitat and reproduction.

	Habitat	Main end-product of nitrogenous excretion	Reproduction
Teleost fish	Fresh water Sea water	Ammonia Ammonia	Eggs without shells
Amphibians	Fresh water before metamorphosis Land and water when adult	Ammonia Urea	Eggs without shells
Reptiles: Turtle, Tortoises	Land and water	Urea and uric acid, some ammonia	Eggs with shells
Crocodiles, Alligators	Land and water	Urea and uric acid, some ammonia	
Snakes, Lizards	Land	Uric acid	
Birds	Land	Uric acid	Eggs with shells
Mammals	Land	Urea	Viviparous

1 Relate the information about the three main excretory products to the habitat and type of reproduction of each of the vertebrate groups given in the table.

54 Excretion

The next table gives further details of excretion in turtles and tortoises.

Habitat of species	Percentage of total non-protein nitrogen as		
	Ammonia	Urea	Uric acid
Wholly in water	20–25	20–25	5
Land and water	6	50–60	5
Land	6	20–30	50
Desert	5	5–10	50–60

2 Say how the information in this table supports your answer to question 1.

Xenopus laevis (South African clawed toad) is an aquatic amphibian. It produces ammonia as its main excretory end-product, but it still survives for some time if its watery habitat dries up. In an investigation into its excretion during times of drought, the excretory products were noted after it had been removed from water, kept on wet grass, and returned to water. Fig. 33 shows the relative proportion of ammonia and urea excreted while in the water, on the grass, and back in water again. A similar change occurs when *Xenopus* aestivates.

Fig. 33. **Relative amounts of ammonia and urea excreted by *Xenopus* in and out of water**

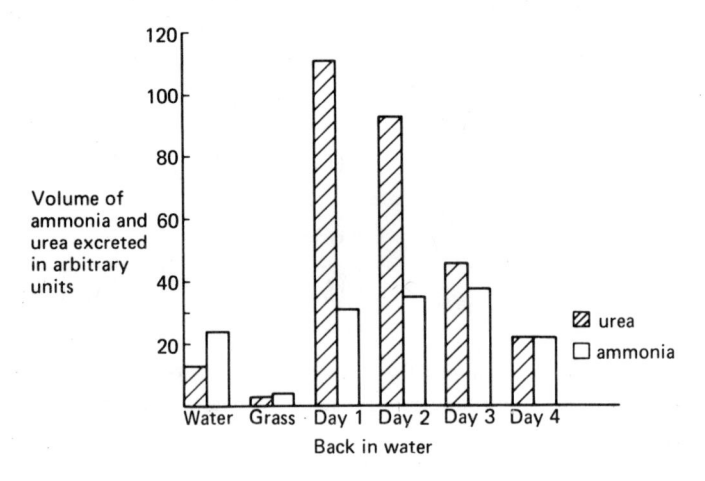

3 Comment on:

a the drop in ammonia on removal from water
b the drop in total excretion on removal from water
c the great increase in total excretion when *Xenopus* is replaced in water.

4.4 The kidney in bony fish

The statements below are about excretion and osmoregulation in teleost fish. These are the fish with which we are most familiar; they have a skeleton made of bone. The statements do not apply to the elasmobranchs (sharks, rays, dog-fish) which have cartilaginous skeletons and a different mode of kidney action.

Using each item of information, and relating the items appropriately to each other, write a short connected account of the role of the kidney in bony fish. Say what you think happens when freshwater species are placed in sea water, and marine species in fresh water.

1 The concentration of salt in the sea is greater than that in the blood of bony fish, which in turn is greater than that in fresh water.

2 Few species of fish are able to make the physiological changes necessary to enable the animal to move from sea water to fresh water or vice versa.

3 Freshwater fish do not drink.

4 Sea fish drink.

5 Freshwater fish produce large amounts of urine.

6 Sea fish produce a small amount of urine.

7 The urine of freshwater fish has a low salt content.

8 The urine of marine fish has a high salt content.

9 When two salt solutions of different concentrations are separated by a differentially permeable membrane, water moves from one side to the other and the salt concentrations on each side of the membrane move towards equality.

4.5 Regulation of body fluids in four invertebrates

For marine animals the maintenance of a satisfactory internal environment should be fairly simple as the concentration of the external environment is similar to that of the animal's own tissue fluids. Animals which live in fresh water, however, have the problem of being surrounded by a watery medium the total salt content of which is much lower than that of the sea, and which also has salts in different proportions from those of the sea.

56 Excretion

During the evolution of aquatic and terrestrial forms of animal life from marine forms, the problem of control of the internal environment must have been one of the first which had to be overcome. Some animals, for example the mammals, can tolerate only very small variations in the osmotic pressure of the internal environment.

This problem concerns some invertebrates which show variations in their ability to withstand osmotic changes in the external environment:

The spider crab, *Maia*, lives in the sea at a depth of over 30 metres.
The shore crab, *Carcinus*, lives in or near estuaries.
The ragworm, *Nereis*, is another estuarine animal (an annelid).

If these three animals are placed in different dilutions of sea water the OP of their body fluids falls according to the graphs shown in Fig. 34.

Fig. 34. **Concentration of body fluid of three species in different dilutions of sea water**

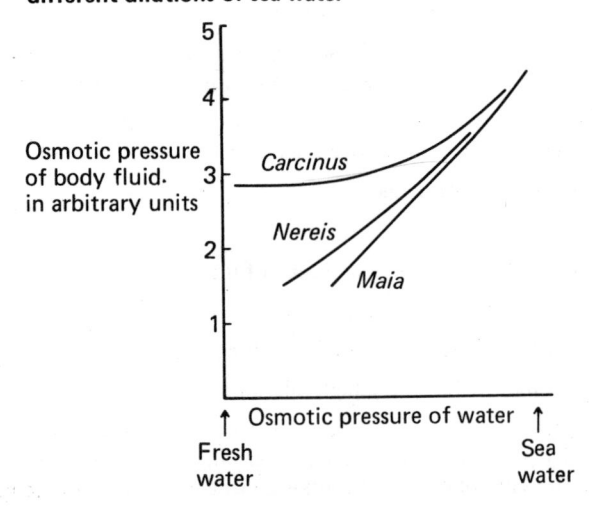

[Graph: Osmotic pressure of body fluid in arbitrary units (y-axis, 1–5) vs Osmotic pressure of water (x-axis, from Fresh water to Sea water), showing curves for Carcinus, Nereis, and Maia]

1 Relate the graphs for these three species to the information given above on their habitats.

	Oxygen uptake per hour in cm^3 g^{-1}
Gammarus pulex: fresh water shrimp	404
G. locusta: marine shrimp	207

Excretion 57

As the salinity of the external water decreases the oxygen consumption of *Carcinus* goes up. The table (page 56) shows data on oxygen uptake per hour, this time for two species of shrimp which are more or less similarly active in their way of life.

2 Comment on these data.

4.6 Contractile vacuoles in protozoa

Contractile vacuoles are found in many protozoa. They fill up with a liquid and then burst, the contents of the vacuole being expelled into the surrounding water. The vacuole then starts to fill up again, and once more bursts.

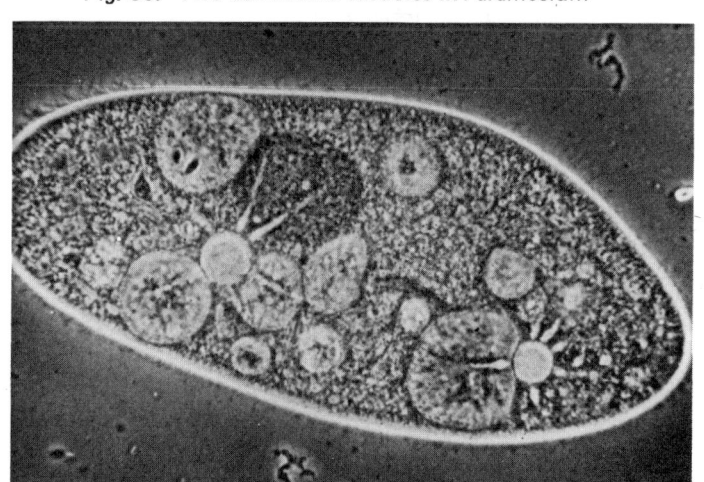

Fig. 35. **Two contractile vacuoles in** *Paramecium*

(Photograph by M.I. Walker, from transparency set TPI, Harris Biological Supplies)

All protozoa which live in fresh water possess one or more contractile vacuoles. They are also present in many marine species, but absent from most protozoan endoparasites.

Freshwater protozoa in their natural environment eliminate more fluid by their contractile vacuole(s) than do the marine forms. To expel an amount of fluid equal in volume to the volume of the animal took between four and 53 minutes for some freshwater species investigated, and between two and five hours for some marine species.

Fig. 36 (page 58) gives a graph typical of results when the action of contractile vacuoles of protozoa is studied in solutions of different concentrations. It shows the rate of elimination for a species of marine *Amoeba* transferred

58 Excretion

from its culture solution of sea water into different dilutions of sea water.

Fig. 36. **Rate of excretion by contractile vacuole in different dilutions of sea water**

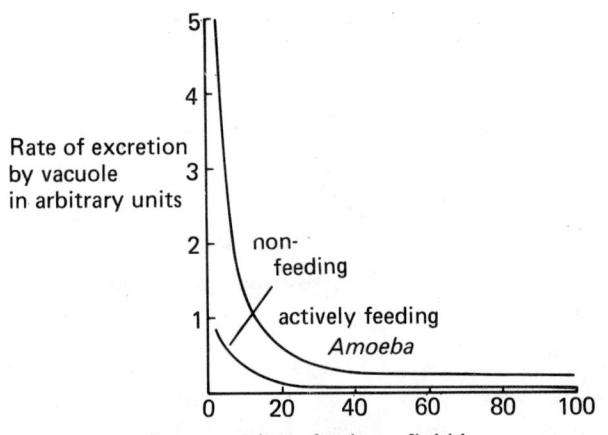

Rate of excretion by vacuole in arbitrary units (y-axis, 0 to 5)
Concentration of culture fluid in percent sea water (x-axis, 0 to 100)

Curves labelled "non-feeding" and "actively feeding Amoeba"

For *Paramecium caudatum,* a freshwater protozoan, placed in different concentrations of salt solutions figures such as those in the table below are obtained.

Percentage NaCl solution	Vacuolar output of fluid in equivalents of body volume per hour
0	4.8
0.5	1.38
0.75	1.08
1.0	0.16

1 From these data, what do you consider to be the function of the contractile vacuole?

2 Where can water enter a protozoan? Compare the two curves of Fig. 36 for one possible point of entry.

There are three possible ways in which the contractile vacuole can fill:

a by hydrostatic pressure across the vacuolar membrane
b by osmosis if the concentration of solutes inside the vacuole is higher

Excretion 59

than that of the surrounding cytoplasm
c by active secretion of water from cytoplasm to vacuole.

3 Below are given some observations which either support or oppose the three theories **a, b** and **c** above. For each, say which theory it supports or opposes and why.

  i The rate at which the vacuole fills seems to be fairly constant regardless of whether it is just starting to fill or is nearly at its maximum size.

 ii Sometimes vacuoles are formed and burst when the animal cell is shrunken.

iii Numerous mitochondria lie close to the vacuolar membrane. There is a rough correlation between the number of mitochondria and the frequency of vacuole action.

 iv Treating a protozoan with a respiratory inhibitor stops the working of the contractile vacuole and the animal swells as it takes up water.

5 Nutrition

5.1 Executives, alcohol and coffee

Given the facts 1 to 5, explain the common observations A, B and C.

1 Stress, aggression and hostility can cause increased acid secretion in the stomach. Depression and fear can cause decreased acid secretion.
2 'Executive' monkeys, trained to press a lever at regular intervals to avoid an electric shock, developed ulcers. In another experiment one monkey had to control a lever which prevented a shock to him and a second monkey by his side. The second monkey had a lever which had no effect. It was the first monkey which developed ulcers.
3 Cutting the vagus nerve to the stomach (vagotomy) reduces the secretion of gastric acid. Vagotomy is often carried out on patients who suffer from gastric ulcers.
4 Fats in the stomach can inhibit its emptying, keeping the food there for a longer time than usual.
5 Tea, coffee or alcohol stimulate gastric secretion.

A There is a higher incidence of ulcers in professional men in responsible positions than in other groups of people.
B Some people drink milk, cream or even olive oil before an alcoholic party.
C Drinking coffee with a meal, or drinking a moderate amount of alcohol, has a beneficial effect on appetite and digestion.

5.2 Diet and amylase activity

The amount of amylase present in the saliva of three groups of people living in Africa was compared, the activity of the amylase being expressed in units per cubic centimetre of saliva:

a The Tswana, whose diet consisted mainly of carbohydrates (sorghum and maize), with irregular small amounts of meat, milk, fruit and vegetables in season. Ninety-two people were examined.

b Thirty-two Europeans, living on a mixed diet.
c Ten Bushmen of the Kalahari Desert, whose diet was mainly carnivorous, consisting of game, birds, snakes and lizards.

The results of the investigation are given in the table.

	Mean activity of salivary amylase in units cm^{-3}
Tswana	248
Europeans	101
Bushmen	22

1 What was the hypothesis under test in this investigation?
2 Do the results support your hypothesis, and if so, how?
3 The differences in salivary activity could have been due to an inherited racial difference, and not to diet. How would you separate out the racial factor?

Searching for Bushmen in the desert and persuading them to change their diet while under surveillance posed certain problems and it was not possible to arrange different diets for any of these three groups of people in their natural surroundings. But five Bushmen, held as court witnesses for three months, were examined. During this period their diet was meal, potatoes, beans and meat, containing far more carbohydrates than they were used to. Their mean amylase activity over the three months on this diet rose to 95 units per cubic centimetre.

4 Does this further evidence suggest that differences in amylase activity is an inherited characteristic or an environmentally caused characteristic?
5 Outline an experimental method which would enable you to determine the activity of salivary amylase.

5.3 Energy requirements

The table (page 63) gives the approximate number of kilojoules and amount of protein needed daily for people at different ages and of different masses.
1 Suggest explanations to account for the differences in energy and protein requirements
   a at different ages
   b between the sexes
   c for pregnant and lactating women.

Fig. 37. **Hunger and malnutrition**

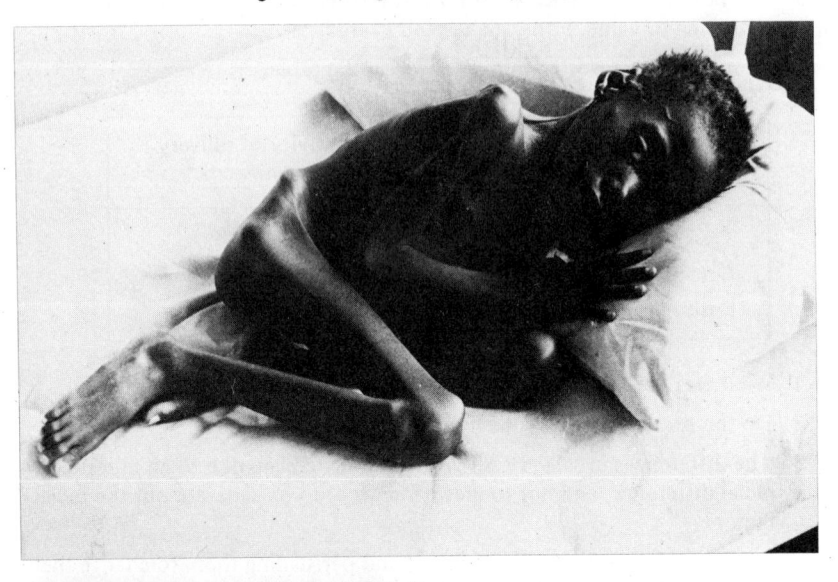

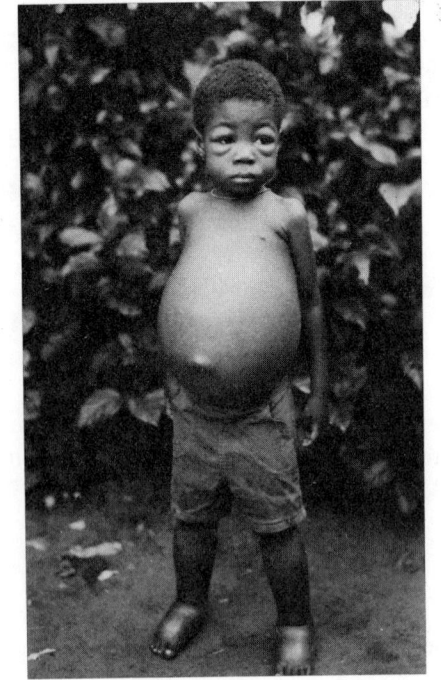

(Photographs by Oxfam)

Nutrition

Age in years	Mass in kg Female	Mass in kg Male	kJ Female	kJ Male	Protein in g Female	Protein in g Male
0–1	8		3 850		20	
1–3	13		5 440		32	
4–6	18		6 690		40	
7–9	24		8 780		52	
10–12	33		9 200	10 040	55	60
13–15	47	45	10 460	12 550	62	75
16–18	53	61	9 620	14 230	58	85
25	58	70	8 780	12 130	58	70
45	58	70	7 950	10 880	58	70
65	58	70	6 690	9 200	58	70
Pregnant woman			+8 370		+20	
Lactating woman			+4 180		+40	

2. The daily requirements would also vary amongst individuals of the same age and sex according to differences in body size, physical activity and environmental temperature. Say why you think these differences would cause different daily requirements.

3. Compare the average daily kilojoule supply in different parts of the world as given in the following table.

	Daily kilojoule supply	% in diet of staple cereals and starchy roots	% in diet of animal products (milk, meat, eggs, fish)
Latin America	10 330	54	17
North America	13 060	25	40
Near East	10 040	71	9
Far East	8 660	73+	5
Africa	9 880	66	11
Europe	12 720	50	21
U.K.	12 720	31	27

64 Nutrition

a What type of countries are those which have excess supplies?
b Even within an area which apparently has sufficient, such as the Near East or Latin America, there can be pockets of severe hunger or malnutrition. Say why you think this can be so.
c Give some causes of energy deficiencies in an underdeveloped country.
d Fig. 37 (page 62) shows one child suffering from malnutrition and one suffering from hunger. What is the difference between hunger and malnutrition?

5.4 Milk and diet

At the start of this century it was realised that what seemed to be a normal diet could nevertheless be deficient in some respects.

F. Gowland Hopkins, in a series of experiments performed between 1906 and 1912, fed young rats different diets. Those represented in Fig. 38 were fed on purified casein (milk protein) only (Curve 1), or casein and one cubic centimetre milk per day for ten days, followed by two (Curve 2) or three (Curve 3) cubic centimetres of milk a day.

Other young rats were fed on a diet of purified casein, starch, cane sugar, lard and salts. They soon stopped growing, lost mass, became ill and died within four weeks, even though the quantity of food they were consuming was ample for growth under normal circumstances. A group of similar rats had this diet supplemented with three cubic centimetres of milk per day, which formed only about four per cent of the total food eaten. On the eighteenth day of the experiment the milk was stopped for this group (Curve 1, on Fig. 39), while another group (Curve 2) on the same diet without the milk started to receive milk. Fig. 39 shows the mass of both groups of rats.

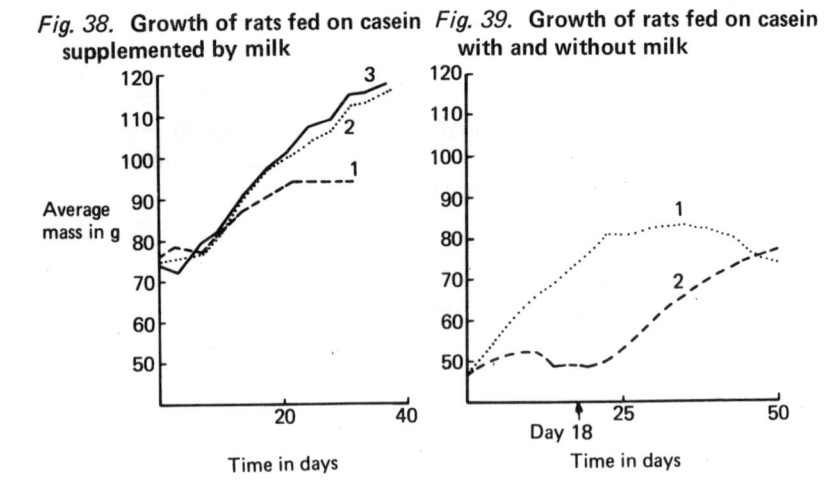

Fig. 38. **Growth of rats fed on casein supplemented by milk**

Fig. 39. **Growth of rats fed on casein with and without milk**

1 What hypothesis was under test in these experiments?
2 Do the results support the hypothesis?
3 What groups of nutrients are present in the unsupplemented diet of the rats shown in Fig. 39?

The table below shows the minimum daily requirement of a number of nutrients, together with a list of some of the things present in milk.

	Daily requirement for adult doing light work	Present in 100 g cow's milk
Kilojoules per day	11 500	276
Protein	80 g	3.3 g
Iron	12.0 mg	0.03 mg
Calcium	0.8 g	0.12 g
Vitamin A and carotene	5 000 iu	150 iu
Vitamin D	–	2 iu
Vitamin B Thiamine	1.1 mg	45 g
Nicotinic acid	11 mg	80 g
Riboflavin	1.6 mg	150 g
Vitamin C	20 mg	2 mg
Water		87.6 g

4 Why would a diet of milk be inadequate for an adult?

5.5 Beri-beri

Beri-beri is a condition still common in parts of the world, characterised by fatigue, muscle weakness, lack of co-ordination of movements, enlargement of the heart, cardiac failure, dropsy or oedema, and finally death. It is caused by lack of vitamin B_1 (thiamine).

Asian sailors who used to have a diet consisting in large measure of polished rice often suffered from beri-beri. In polishing the rice, the outer layers (husk) are removed leaving the sort of rice we buy in packets in Britain. The Japanese surgeon, Takaki, who was director of the Tokyo naval hospital, discovered (in 1884) that beri-beri did not occur if the sailors ate barley instead of rice, particularly if the barley was supplemented by meat, fresh vegetables, and fish.

1 Considering the rice diet, construct two different hypotheses which Takaki could have put forward to explain the cause of beri-beri.

66 Nutrition

Later (1896) a Dutchman, Eijkman, was sent to the East Indies by the Dutch Government to investigate beri-beri in the native population. Near a hospital which housed a number of beri-beri patients he saw chickens with a condition which seemed similar to human beri-beri: they had drooping wings and walked unsteadily. The chickens had been fed on food scraps dropped in the kitchen and dining areas of the hospital. Eijkman's hypothesis was that beri-beri was an infectious illness caused by micro-organisms, and not due to poor nutrition. This was at a time when Pasteur's work on micro-organisms was uppermost in people's minds, and bacteria were often considered to be the only cause of disease.

2 Suggest at least two approaches towards testing Eijkman's hypothesis that beri-beri was an infectious illness.

Eijkman's bacteriological experiments on the chickens were stopped by hospital officials aghast at the waste of the polished rice fed to them, which had cost money to have the outer layers removed. The chickens were then given unpolished rice, regarded as unsuitable for human consumption. On this diet the chickens showing beri-beri rapidly recovered, and other chickens put with them while they were ill did not get beri-beri.

3 Which hypothesis is disproved by this observation?

In a survey to discover if unpolished rice had a beneficial effect on people suffering from beri-beri, Eijkman gathered data from a large number of prisons in Java, involving a total of 279 629 prisoners. In some parts of the country, depending on local dietary customs, prisoners ate polished rice, and in others half-polished (where one outer layer, the hull, had been removed but not the other, the cuticle) or unpolished rice.

Some of the data collected:

On a diet of half-polished rice, beri-beri occurred in only one out of thirty-five prisons, or one prisoner per ten thousand.

On a diet of polished rice, beri-beri occurred in thirty-six out of fifty-one prisons, or one prisoner per thirty-nine.

In thirteen prisons where both polished and half-polished rice was given, beri-beri occurred in six of them, or one prisoner per four hundred and sixteen.

4 How do these figures support your answer to question 3?

5.6 Fluoride and tooth decay

Fluorine is present in animal tissues in amounts ranging from 0.2 to 1.5 mg per 100 g dry material. Bones and teeth contain larger amounts of 20 to 30 mg per 100 g ash. Fluorine is particularly incorporated into the dentine and enamel of the teeth. When the amount incorporated is large, the enamel has a discoloured, mottled appearance: bands of brown pigmentation between chalkish white patches. A normal diet provides some fluoride, and in some areas the drinking water also contains fluoride. A lot of fluoride in the water (8 ppm) causes the mottling mentioned above, but these teeth are almost free from dental caries (tooth decay). The amount of fluoride in the water supply varies, depending on the source of the water. Some will have none.

The table gives the number of decayed teeth per child of average age thirteen years, by the side of the amount of fluoride in the drinking water in various parts of America.

Fluoride in water supply (ppm)	0.0	0.125	0.25	0.5	0.85	1.0	1.35	1.5	2.0	2.5
Approximate number decayed teeth per child	8.0	8.2	6.3	4.2	3.3	3.0	2.8	2.6	2.5	2.4

1 Graph these results.
2 How do you think the figures were obtained?

In order to gather more data, a number of towns in Britain had fluoride added to their drinking water to bring the level up to 1 ppm. Each trial town was paired with a control town which received no added fluoride. Dental caries in the experimental towns was reduced by about 60 per cent.

	No caries				10 or more decayed, extracted or filled teeth			
	Boys		Girls		Boys		Girls	
	1965	1972	1965	1972	1965	1972	1965	1972
3 years old	44.8	65.7	38.6	74.5	9.8	2.7	7.9	1.7
5 years old	21.6	32.7	25.5	40.3	9.0	2.8	8.5	1.9
8 years old	6.3	18.3	4.9	21.3	9.4	2.7	6.3	0.5

68 Nutrition

In 1964, Birmingham added fluoride to its drinking water to give a fluoride level of 1 ppm. The percentages of sample groups of children of various ages with decayed or extracted teeth are shown in the last table.

3 Using the data given, evaluate the hypothesis that increasing amounts of fluoride in the drinking water helps prevent tooth decay.

There was, however, and still is, opposition from some people to the proposal that fluoride should be added to water to help reduce dental decay. Two points put forward against the proposal to add fluoride are

a it is an arbitrary action by those in authority. The individual who has no control over the water which comes from his tap is being coerced by government controlled means and this constitutes an invasion of a person's natural rights,

b fluoride is harmful.

4 Discuss these two points, and put forward arguments to counter them.

5 Perhaps the most satisfactory way of supplying fluoride for developing teeth in areas which lack it is to provide fluoride tablets for parents to give to their children, should they wish to do so. Would this answer the 'mass medication' criticism made against adding fluoride to the water supply?

5.7 The production of veal

Many male calves born to cows which have been bred for their milk potential are not suitable for rearing as beef, and pose a problem about what to do with them. A lot are kept for three months before being slaughtered and their flesh sold as veal. The fashion is for people to want veal as pale in colour as possible, but the pale muscles of a newly born calf soon darken with exercise (due to the formation of myoglobin), food (iron is necessary for the formation of haemoglobin), and age.

At one time, intensive methods of producing veal by keeping calves under conditions in which they were allowed little exercise and provided with a strictly controlled diet prompted a great deal of public concern. It was said that these methods were cruel and harmful to the animals. This led to research being undertaken on problems connected with such methods and the subject was debated on occasions in the House of Commons, leading eventually to the banning of some of the practices employed.

Some of the practices which **used** to be employed for the intensive production of veal are given below. They were used with two ends in view: to cause a rapid increase in mass and to make the flesh as pale as possible.

a Up to fifty years ago, suckling calves were nicked in the neck vein once a fortnight, and some blood allowed to drain away.

b Black pepper was given to make the calves drink more milk.

Nutrition 69

c Calves were fed exclusively on whole or skimmed milk long after weaning.
d Calves were kept in complete darkness.
e Calves were not allowed to move, either being tethered on a short rope, or having their heads held between two vertical wooden bars.
f The temperature was kept at 15 to 18 °C.
g No water was allowed between feeds.
h No straw was allowed, the calves standing on wooden slats.
i No ungalvanised iron was used, for example, for buckets.

1 What do you think was the reasoning behind the adoption of each practice?

2 Say whether you think it was sound reasoning or not.

3 Do you consider any of these practices cruel and, if so, why?

4 Is it possible to assess what is cruel to an animal?

5 One of the arguments put forward to justify intensive farming methods is that the animals grow rapidly, showing marked increases in mass, and can therefore be considered 'happy'. Do you think this is a reasonable definition of 'happiness' under the circumstances?

6 Digestion

6.1 Control of gastric secretion

The stomach lining contains glands which produce gastric juice, mucus and hydrochloric acid. Pepsinogen produced by the peptic cells in the glands is converted to the enzyme pepsin by the action of hydrochloric acid. The lining of the pylorus (part of the stomach) also secretes a hormone, gastrin, which stimulates the secretion of hydrochloric acid. The stomach has a very rich blood supply, and is also served by branches of the vagus nerve. Fig. 40 shows the chief regions of the stomach.

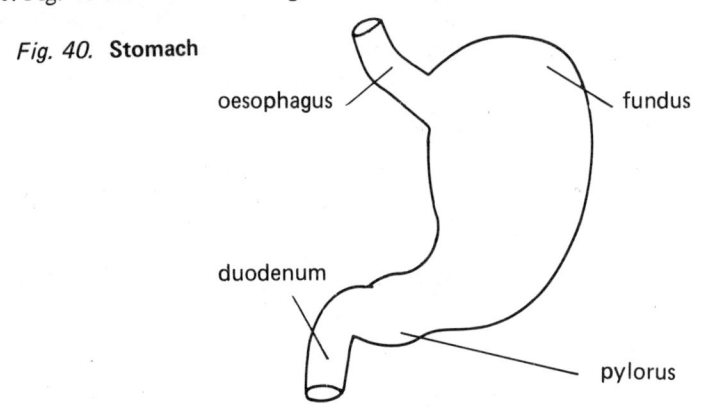

Fig. 40. **Stomach**

I Investigations to determine what controls the gastric secretions have been performed on dogs, and the experimental work given below (1 to 8) relates to these investigations. The conclusions drawn from these experiments are given in **A** to **H**. For each conclusion say which piece or pieces of evidence (1 to 8) support it.

Evidence

1 a When food is placed in the mouth, even if it never reaches the stomach (sham feeding), or at the sight or smell of food, the stomach secretes gastric juice within five minutes.
  b This secretion stops soon after the stimulus is stopped. After normal feeding, the secretion continues for three to four hours.

Digestion

2 If the vagus nerve from the brain to the stomach is cut, **1a** no longer happens. But if the cut end of the part of the vagus still attached to the stomach is stimulated electrically, the stomach secretes gastric juice.

3 **a** The presence of undigested meat, if introduced surgically directly into the stomach without passing through the mouth and oesophagus, does not cause secretion.

   b If, however, meat is introduced together with gastric juice, or if a solution of already digested meat is injected into the stomach, secretion soon starts and continues for two to three hours. This happens even when the vagus is cut.

4 Part of the stomach can be cut off, made into a pouch, and transplanted into the abdominal region where it acquires a blood supply but has no nerve connection. If predigested meat is then put into the main part of the animal's stomach, or if it is fed normally, the pouch also starts to secrete after about a quarter of an hour and continues to do so for about two hours.

5 **a** A pouch is made and transplanted as in **4**. In addition the remainder of the stomach is removed from the gut and sewn up, thus cutting its nerves but maintaining its blood supply. Again, predigested meat put inside the main part of the stomach causes it and the pouch to secrete, even if the pouch lining is anaesthetised. When the lining of the main part of the stomach is anaesthetised there is no secretion in either. The anaesthetic could prevent the stomach wall from secreting a substance or prevent absorption of a substance.

   b Predigested meat given by mouth causes secretion in both stomach and pouch, even when anaesthetised.

6 The pure hormone, gastrin, injected into a blood vessel causes gastric secretion.

7 In experiments to find out which part of the stomach is receptive, different parts were removed.

   a When the pylorus was removed, secretion fell markedly.

   b When nearly the whole stomach was made into a pouch and transplanted elsewhere, leaving the oesophagus and small intestine connected only by

   i the pylorus: there was secretion inside the transplanted pouch

   ii the fundus: very little secretion inside the transplanted pouch.

   c If, in this position, the pylorus is connected so that food and the products of its digestion cannot enter it, secretion falls markedly.

8 Even when the whole stomach is removed and transplanted elsewhere in the body, there is still a small amount of gastric secretion when the products of digestion reach the small intestine.

Digestion

Conclusions

A There are at least two phases of secretion of gastric juice. The first is a reflex (simple or conditioned) caused by the taste, smell or sight of food; the second is due to the presence of food in the stomach.

B The first stimulation mentioned in **A** travels via the vagus nerve to the stomach.

C Secretion is stimulated by something travelling in the blood:
  i a hormone *or*
  ii the products of digestion.

D i The stomach itself produces the hormone (gastrin) when the products of digestion start to appear.
  ii Hormone production is not stimulated by undigested meat alone.

E The mechanism seems to be that secretion is started by the taste, smell or sight of food through nervous stimulation of the stomach, and is then maintained for two to four hours by a hormone produced by the stomach when digestion products accumulate.

F The pyloric region produces the hormone.

G The stimulus to hormone secretion by the pylorus is the presence of the products of digestion.

H There is a third phase of gastric secretion: an intestinal phase. This is probably due to the release of a hormone from the intestinal wall caused by the presence of the products of digestion.

II Write an account of the control of gastric secretion under the three headings commonly used:
  a cephalic
  b gastric
  c intestinal.

6.2 Control of pancreatic secretion

The secretion of pancreatic juice is controlled by mechanisms somewhat similar to those controlling gastric secretion (problem **6.1**).

Given the following pieces of evidence, construct a brief account of the control of pancreatic secretion.

1 The flow of pancreatic juice starts one to two minutes after a meal, and may start in response to the sight or smell of food.

Digestion 73

2 Stimulation of the branch of the vagus nerve which goes to the pancreas causes the secretion of pancreatic juice.

3 Cutting the vagus nerve causes such a very small reduction in total enzyme production by the pancreas that normal digestion is not interfered with.

4 Peptones (products of protein digestion) put into the intestine cause increased pancreatic secretion.

5 Hydrochloric acid put into the intestine causes copious secretion of pancreatic juice. This happens even when the vagus nerve is cut.

6 Acid extracts of the intestine lining, injected in the blood stream, cause pancreatic secretion. This happens even when the vagus nerve is cut, or when the pancreas is transplanted to another region of the body.

7 Peptones, amino acids and fats put into the intestine cause the secretion of the hormone secretin by the intestine.

8 Pure secretin, injected into the blood system, causes profuse pancreatic secretion in less than a minute.

6.3 The digestion and absorption of fat

Bile salts contribute towards the digestion of fats to fatty acids by helping to emulsify them, and thus there is a larger surface area for the fat digesting enzymes to work on. However, if the bile duct is tied, or the bile prevented from reaching the intestine, for example by gall stones, fatty acids appear as usual in the faeces, so presumably digestion has taken place without bile. A further role of bile salts is in the absorption of fatty acids from the intestine: if olive oil is put into a tied-off loop of intestine with lipase also present, the oil is digested to oleic acid, but the oleic acid is absorbed only if bile salts are also present in the loop. This effect is caused by the ability of bile salts to form water-soluble complexes with fatty acids.

1 Why do you think a water-soluble compound would be more readily absorbed than a fat?

In an experiment into fatty acid absorption, oleic acid and bile salts were put into a number of intestinal loops. Glycerol and/or phosphate, or glyceryl phosphate were added to the loops as shown in the table. Iodoacetate was also added to one loop. Iodoacetate is an inhibitor of glycolysis in respiration, a process in which phosphorylation plays a basic part. The results are given overleaf.

74 Digestion

Contents of intestinal loop	Relative amounts of oleic acid absorbed in six hours
Oleic acid and bile salt	2.9
Oleic acid and glycerol and bile salt	2.5
Oleic acid and phosphate and bile salt	1.0
Oleic acid and glycerol and phosphate and bile salt	4.9
Oleic acid and glyceryl phosphate and bile salt	7.3
Oleic acid and glyceryl phosphate and bile salt and iodoacetate	0.0

As an interpretation of these results it was suggested that a compound of the fatty acid with glycerol and phosphate was formed. Unlike fatty acids such compounds are soluble in water.

2   What three pieces of evidence from the table support the view that the formation of such a compound facilitates the absorption of fats?

It was also suggested that the process of absorption of fatty acids could involve phosphorylation.

3   What evidence from the table supports this suggestion?

6.4   Digestion of cellulose

Three families of termites have bacteria and flagellates (unicellular protozoa) in their digestive tracts. The termites can live on pure cellulose, and a cellulose-digesting enzyme (cellulase) can be extracted from the hind gut contents. If the flagellates are removed the insects soon die, but if the flagellates are restored in time they recover. Without flagellates they will survive if fed on glucose or predigested cellulose.

1   From the evidence here, what do you think might be the function of the flagellates in the insect gut?

2   What name is given to the relationship shown here between flagellate and insect?

Ruminant animals such as cows, sheep and goats living on grass do not themselves produce a cellulase, but the rumen usually contains both bacteria and ciliated protozoa. In a number of investigations lambs and goats had their protozoa removed (by starvation and injections of copper sulphate into the paunch), and later showed no nutritional deficiency. It is therefore assumed that it is the bacteria which are responsible for the digestion of cellulose.

3 What could be the relationship between the protozoa and the ruminant?

6.5 Structure and function of the intestine and alveoli

The functions of the intestine are:
a the secretion of digestive juices containing enzymes, and the secretion of mucus which provides a lining to the intestine,
b the absorption of digested food,
c peristaltic movement which propels the contents of the intestine along.

1 Say how the structure of the intestine allows each of these functions to be carried out. Figs. 41 A, B and C are photographs to show the microscopic structure of the intestine.

Fig. 41. **Intestinal structure**

A TS of part of small intestine, LP, injected, unstained. Note the villi and their blood supply, and the muscular intestinal wall.

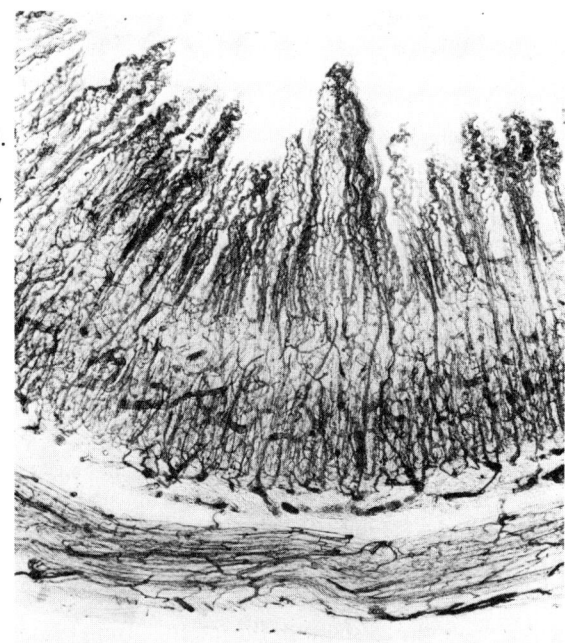

(Photograph by John Haller, Harris Biological Supplies)

76 Digestion

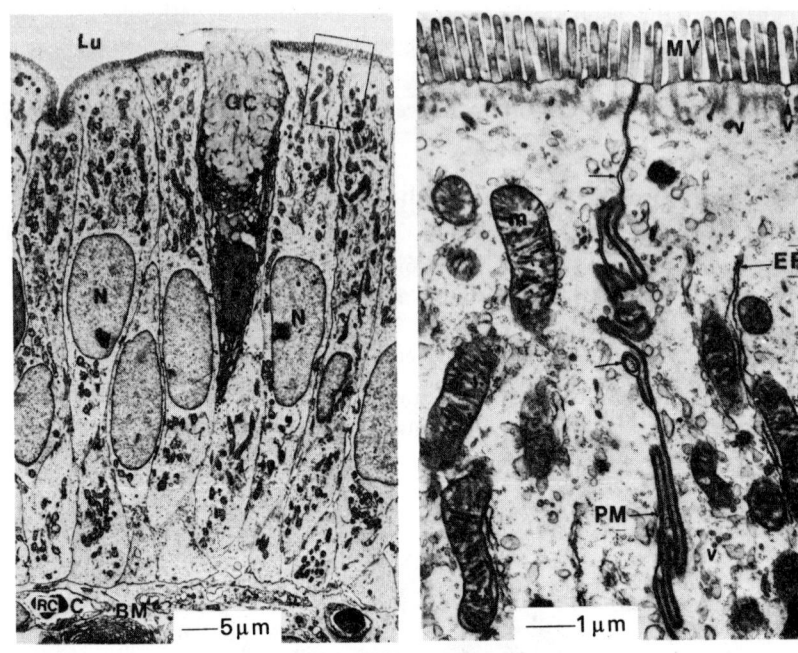

Fig. 41. **Intestinal structure (cont'd)**

B EM of whole thickness of columnar epithelium of small intestine. GC: goblet cell discharging mucus into the lumen. RC: red cell. C: capillary. BM: basement membrane. N: nucleus. Lu: lumen.

C EM of superficial parts of two adjacent columnar cells of intestine (from B). MV: microvilli which make up the brush border. v: pinocytic vesicle. ER: endoplasmic reticulum. m: mitochondrion. PM: plasma membrane showing interdigitation at the arrows and elsewhere.

(Figs. 41B and 41C: Photographs by J.H. Kugler, from transparency set EMI, Harris Biological Supplies)

Like the intestine lining, the alveoli of the lungs provide a vast surface area, but this time it is oxygen which is absorbed and water and carbon dioxide which are released. The structure of the alveoli is quite different from that of the intestine, but it is equally well adapted for its function of gaseous exchange. Fig. 42 shows a section through lung alveoli.

2 Compare the alveoli with the intestine from the point of view of structure related to function.

Fig. 42. **Section through lung alveoli, × 375**

Note red blood cells inside capillaries, thin alveolus wall, elastic fibres

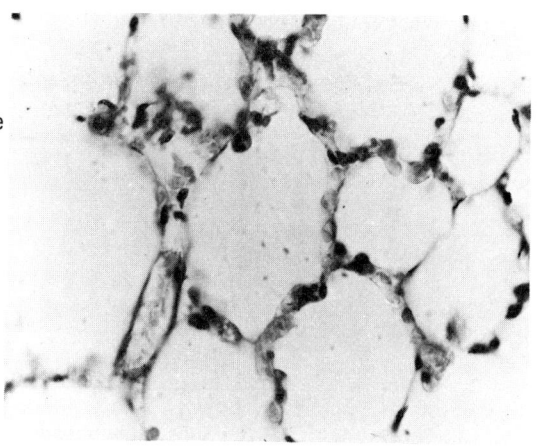

(Photograph by John Haller, Harris Biological Supplies)

6.6 Enzyme action under different conditions

In experiments with an enzyme from a mammalian gut the two curves labelled A in Figs. 43 and 44 were obtained.

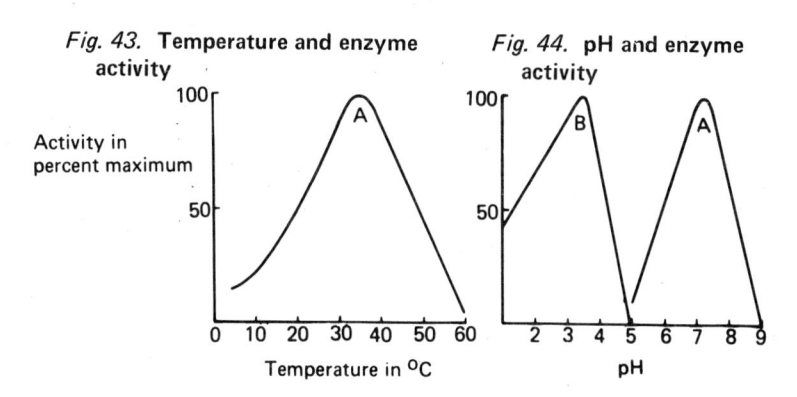

Fig. 43. **Temperature and enzyme activity**

Fig. 44. **pH and enzyme activity**

1 At what temperature and pH would you perform experiments with this enzyme for optimum activity?

2 In Fig. 43 the amount of product rises between 10° C and 30 °C. Is the increase normal for chemical reactions, where $Q_{10} = 2$?

3 Why does the activity of the enzyme drop over 35·°C?

4 Curve B on Fig. 44 shows the pH curve for another mammalian enzyme. Give the names of two enzymes the activity of which could be represented by curves A and B on Fig. 44.

78 Digestion

5 Fig. 45 shows the action of an enzyme at different substrate concentrations. What could be beginning to limit the rate of reaction at X?

Fig. 45. **Substrate concentration and enzyme activity**

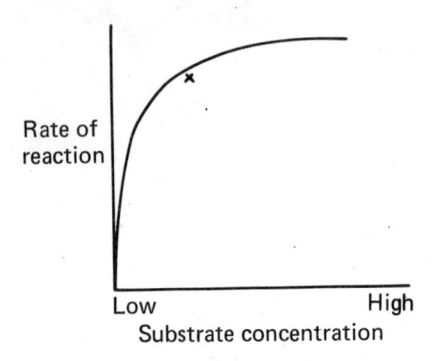

6 Fig. 46 shows the amount of product formed with an excess of substrate, plotted against time in one case and enzyme concentration in the other. Which curve is which? Give the reasons for your answer.

Fig. 46. **Enzyme activity related to two factors**

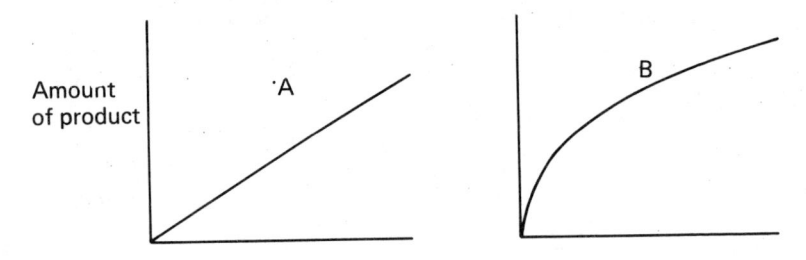

6.7 An enzyme experiment

Two substances in solution, X and Y, join together slowly to produce the compound XY at normal laboratory temperatures. Both a metallic element and an enzyme can catalyse the reaction to the same extent. An experiment is set up with four flasks, each containing the same amount of a mixture of solutions X and Y.

Flask A contains the solutions X and Y only.
Flask B contains equal and small amounts of both the metallic catalyst and the enzyme.
Flask C contains twice as much enzyme as Flask B, but no metallic catalyst.

Flask D contains twice as much metallic catalyst as Flask B, but no enzyme.

Flask E contains twice as much metallic catalyst and enzyme as Flask B.

Give your reasons as you answer the following questions.

In which flask or flasks would you expect the rate of reaction to be greatest:

1 at a temperature of 20 °C
2 at a temperature of 60 °C
3 if the pH of solutions X and Y is changed
4 if twice as much X and Y is put in at the start of the experiment?

In which flask or flasks would you expect the rate of reaction to:

5 slow down with time
6 increase if more of the two substrates is added when the rate of reaction has slowed down?

6.8 The liver and blood sugar

Claude Bernard, a Frenchman, was a great physiologist of the nineteenth century. Among other work, he elucidated the role of the liver in glucose metabolism.

The first part of the following data and questions covers some of his work which resulted in a paper in 1855.

Bernard observed that in carnivorous animals whose food contains no sugar, sugar (glucose) is always present in the liver and blood.

1 What conclusion may be drawn from this observation?

2 Bernard also noted

a In carnivorous animals the blood which enters the liver by the hepatic portal vein contains no sugar. The blood which leaves the liver by the hepatic veins contains appreciable amounts of sugar.
b In other animals, and particularly those which are fasting, the blood of the hepatic vein contains more sugar than is present in the blood taken simultaneously from the hepatic portal vein.
c If the liver of a fasting dog is removed the blood sugar falls rapidly, the animal has convulsions and is nearly dead five hours after the removal of the liver. A fasting dog with its liver intact has normal levels of blood sugar.

What conclusion may be drawn from these observations?

80 Digestion

In Bernard's time the belief was that the liver contributed nothing to the secretion of sugar, but that it acted in some way on the blood which passed through it so that the sugar was formed directly in the blood.

Bernard's experiment to investigate this hypothesis was as follows. An adult dog, fed only on meat for several days, was killed. The liver was immediately removed and while still warm and before the blood had time to clot, was washed with cold water through the portal vein. The water flowed through the liver very rapidly expelling the blood through the hepatic vein in a strong continuous jet. The liver was washed continuously for forty minutes by which time it was bloodless and the emerging water colourless.

At the start of the washing both liver and emerging blood had contained sugar. At the end neither the liver nor the emerging water did. The sugar-free liver was left in a closed jar at room temperature for twenty-four hours, when it was found to contain abundant sugar.

3 What conclusions may be drawn from this investigation?

Further investigation showed that **a** boiling the liver after washing completely prevented the formation of any new sugar, **b** the powdery substance obtained by passing fresh, partly washed liver through a strainer to remove vessels and nerves, washing with cold alcohol to remove any sugar, and then drying, was able to form sugar when placed in water, even after being kept for months. If the powder was first boiled in water, no sugar was produced.

4 What seems to be bringing about the conversion of something in the liver to sugar?

The liver then produces something which can be made into glucose. This precursor is called glycogen. The next section considers a possible source of the glycogen.

More recent investigations have shown that, after a meal of sugars and other carbohydrates

a immediately after the meal the level of sugar in the circulating blood is lower than would be expected if all the sugar were available in the blood,
b some nine hours after the meal the level is higher than would be expected. This coincides with Bernard's point **2b** where sugar seems to be added to the blood,
c the level of blood sugar in the hepatic portal vein entering the liver is higher than that in the hepatic vein leaving the liver.
d At the same time there is no increase in glucose in the liver but
e the concentration of glycogen rises in the liver as the glucose level between the hepatic portal and hepatic veins drops.
f Hours after the meal, the glycogen concentration of the liver drops and

there is more glucose in the blood in the hepatic vein than in that in the hepatic portal vein.

g If the liver is diseased the level of blood sugar in the circulating blood is higher than in **a**.

5 The following paragraph contains the conclusions which may be drawn from this evidence. At each point where there is a * give the letter of the piece or pieces of evidence which support the preceding phrase.

The sugar which has disappeared may be destroyed in the body or excreted (*) but it seems more likely that it is stored (*). From the evidence given here the storage seems to be in the liver (*), but it is not stored there as glucose (*), but probably as glycogen (*), which is converted to glucose (*).

It is now known that the 'sugar former', glycogen, can be formed continually in the liver from a variety of food materials. The glycogen so formed may accumulate in liver cells, or be converted to glucose and pass into the blood. If more glycogen is formed than is converted, then the glycogen store in the liver increases. If the reverse happens, then the liver store is depleted. In fasting, the liver converts its glycogen into glucose (glycogenolysis), with the result noted by Bernard — there is more sugar in the blood leaving the liver than in the blood entering it. Even at the end of ten or twelve days without food, there are still traces of glycogen in the liver.

The liver responds then to a changed blood sugar level in such a way as to restore it to normal. At blood glucose levels of about 0.7 g dm^{-3} blood the production and liberation of glucose are about equal. The liver thus functions as a sort of 'glucostat', maintaining a constant level of circulating glucose.

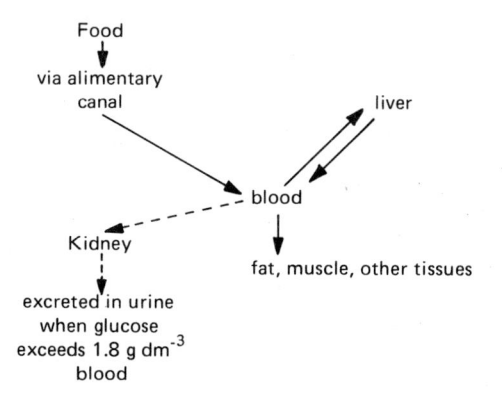

```
                    Food
                     ↓
              via alimentary
                 canal                    liver
                      ↘                ↗
                         ⇌ blood ⇌
                 ↗            ↓
           Kidney      fat, muscle, other tissues
              ↓
        excreted in urine
          when glucose
        exceeds 1.8 g dm$^{-3}$
             blood
```

Glycogen is also present in most other body tissues, particularly in skeletal muscle.

6.9 Diabetes

The normal level of glucose in the blood is 0.7 g dm^{-3}. Unlike the excess products of protein digestion, excess glucose is not immediately excreted but when blood sugar levels are very high, exceeding 1.8 g dm^{-3}, sugar is excreted by the kidneys and appears in the urine.

1 Suggest a function of the unexcreted but excess glucose.

The disease diabetes mellitus is characterised by the appearance of glucose in the urine, as well as a number of other symptoms which rapidly or eventually lead to death if the disease is untreated.

Fig. 47. **Glucose tolerance curves**

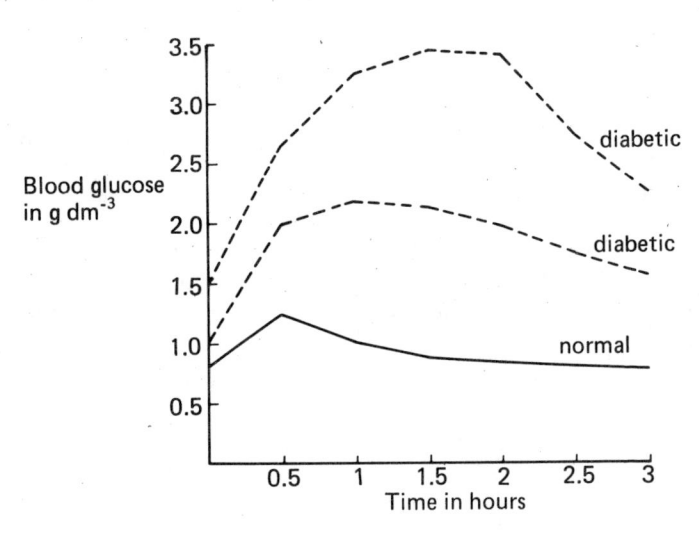

In man, the predisposition to diabetes is inherited as a mendelian recessive trait. Over twenty per cent of the relatives of diabetic patients have abnormal glucose tolerance curves, compared with less than one per cent of those without a family history of the disease. Incipient diabetes may be brought on by overweight, extreme stress or pregnancy.

A glucose tolerance test can be given to a person with suspected diabetes. The person eats and drinks nothing for twelve hours, and then drinks fifty grams of glucose in water. After the drink the amount of blood sugar is measured every thirty minutes for three hours.

2 What is the reason for not allowing the person any food or drink for twelve hours before the glucose tolerance test?

Fig. 47 gives some glucose tolerance curves for normal and diabetic people.

A normal person has insulin, produced by the Islets of Langerhans in the pancreas, circulating in his or her blood. It is the action of insulin which causes the fall in blood glucose noted in the normal curve in the figure. In diabetics, as the two curves show, glucose accumulates in the blood.

3 From the diabetic curves, does a diabetic produce too much or too little insulin?

4 How would you show that

a the pancreas is the organ responsible for the production of insulin

b the pancreas cells concerned act by producing an internal secretion which passes into the blood, and not by modifying the blood itself as it passes through the tissue

c the active substance is insulin

d insulin is a substance which does not pass through the pancreatic duct with the pancreatic enzymes?

It was Banting and Best, in 1921, who showed that pancreatic tissue could be used to prepare a substance which could be used to treat diabetics. All previous attempts to prepare such a substance from pancreatic tissue had been unsuccessful, the products being either inactive or toxic. Banting and Best, however, used pancreas in which the acinar tissue (which produces the digestive enzymes of the pancreas) had degenerated. This was done by tying the pancreatic duct of a dog, and seven to ten weeks later, killing the dog and removing the pancreas. The acinar tissue had degenerated completely, but the Islets of Langerhans were intact and presumably working as the dog did not suffer from diabetes.

5 Suggest a reason for the inactivation of insulin when the extract of whole pancreas was used.

7 Nerves and Muscles

7.1 Conduction in nerves
I General properties of nerves

In work on nerves a nerve-muscle preparation, the gastrocnemius muscle from the hind leg of a frog with the sciatic nerve attached, is usually used. Stimulation of the nerve is usually by an electric current, convenient because its timing, duration and intensity can be controlled and it causes no injury to the nerve. The response to the stimulus is seen in the contraction or twitch of the muscle.

The list of observations **1** to **4** summarises some of the early work on conduction of nervous impulses. The conclusions drawn from these observations are given in **A** to **D**. Say which observation supports each conclusion given.

1. It is possible to move a part of the body, for example a toe, without the contraction of any other muscles, for example in the leg, and the sensations from the toe are not confused with those from the leg.
2. Unless the stimulus of a nerve reaches or passes a certain strength, the muscle does not contract at all.
3. The current stimulates a contraction in the muscle only when it starts or stops, not when it flows continuously.
4. A stimulus applied to the nerve at a point near to the muscle causes a twitch sooner than one applied at a point some distance from the muscle. The twitch is further delayed if the nerve is cold. In man conduction slows by a factor of 1.7 for a drop in temperature of 10 °C.

A. A sudden change in stimulus is more effective than a slow alteration or a continuous flow.
B. There is insulation between nerve fibres, preventing the passage of a stimulus from one fibre across to another.
C. Conduction along a nerve takes a little time (50 metres per second in the fastest fibres in human limbs, 25 metres per second in a frog).
D. The nerve has a threshhold, and it does not conduct unless the threshhold is reached or exceeded.

II Propagation of nerve impulse along the fibre

5 Does the nerve impulse get the energy it needs for propagation along the fibre

a from a starting stimulus (as a bullet from a gun) or
b locally as it goes along (like a flame along a gunpowder trail)?

Consider this evidence before you answer:

In a long nerve the stimulus does not decrease or get slower as it passes along.

To get the same muscle contraction a stimulus applied to the end of a nerve need not be larger than one applied nearer to the muscle.

The impulse does not go faster if a large stimulus is given.

Cooling of a small section of the nerve causes the impulse to go more slowly along that section, but when it passes through and gets to the nerve at the normal temperature it goes at its original rate.

6 Do the following observations support the conclusion that the nerve impulse is an all or nothing affair, and that information and instructions are different because of the differing *frequency* (speed with which impulses follow each other) of the impulses, not differing size? If so, how?

a If increasingly strong stimuli are given to a nerve, once threshold has been reached the muscle contractions increase in size for some time.
b On stimulating with increasingly stronger stimuli the nerve of a very small muscle (the cutaneous dorsi of the frog) which consists of only eight or nine fibres, the size of the muscle contraction does not increase smoothly. Instead it increases in a number of steps which is not more than the number of fibres in the muscle.
c Some invertebrates have giant nerve fibres, up to one millimetre in diameter. A single giant fibre when stimulated with an increasingly strong current shows an action potential (see below) of a certain height once its threshold is reached. The height does not vary regardless of how strong the stimulus becomes, neither can a height of less than the first be obtained.

III Action potential

If two electrodes placed on the surface of a nerve fibre are connected through an amplifier to a cathode ray oscilloscope, no potential difference is observed. However, if one electrode is put inside the fibre a potential difference across the cell membrane is observed. When the fibre is not conducting an impulse this is called the *resting potential* and is about 90 millivolts (mV) for vertebrate nerves. The inside of the cell is negatively charged relative to the outside, so the resting potential is expressed as a negative potential, -90 mV.

86   Nerves and Muscles

When a fibre is stimulated a brief wave of negativity travels along the fibre from the stimulating electrode. This wave is called the *action potential*. It is larger than the resting potential, not only reaching zero potential, but also overshooting it by about 30 to 40 mV, the inside becoming positive to the outside. The change from resting to action potential and back again gives a tracing on the oscilloscope like that below.

Fig. 48. **Resting and action potentials from a single nerve fibre**

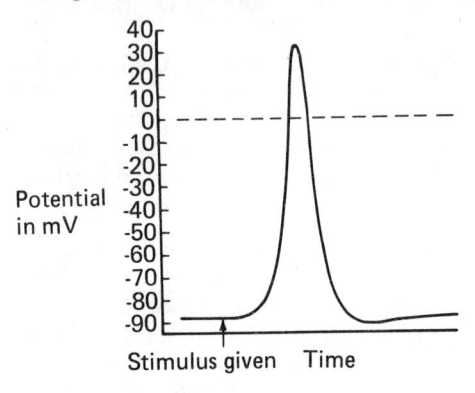

7   It is now known that nervous conduction is electrical, but in the early days of research on the problem the question not resolved was:
    Are the action potential and the nervous impulse which passes down the nerve and makes the muscle contract the same thing? They have the same threshhold, go along at the same velocity, and if the nerve is cooled they are both blocked at the same time, but this evidence does not prove that they *are* the same. Suggest an alternative hypothesis.

8   What evidence given so far supports the theory of electrical conduction?

7.2   Nerve-muscle preparations

A frog's nerve-muscle (see Fig. 49) preparation provides one of the classical exercises in experimental physiology. It usually consists of the gastrocnemius muscle from the frog's hind leg together with the sciatic nerve which supplies it. The knee joint is fixed and the muscle tendon attached to a lever. When the nerve or muscle is stimulated electrically, the muscle contracts and shortens, and the lever is pulled up, its tip making a mark on smoked paper attached to a drum. During the experiment a time marker also writes on the smoked paper.

With a single adequate electrical impulse, the muscle gives a single *twitch:* a brief period of contraction followed by relaxation. Fig. 50 is a diagram of a tracing obtained of a single muscle twitch.

Nerves and Muscles 87

Fig. 49. **Frog nerve—muscle preparation from above**

The nerve, on the left of the preparation, extends upwards to the electrodes. The other end of the muscle is attached to a lever.

(Photograph by John Haller, Harris Biological Supplies)

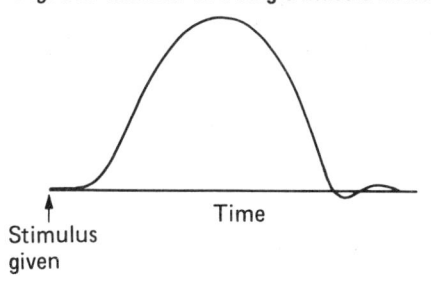

Fig. 50. Record of a single muscle twitch

↑
Stimulus   Time
given

1 On this tracing mark what you consider to be
   a the latent period during which the impulse is travelling from the point of stimulation to the muscle
   b the period of contraction
   c the period of relaxation
   d the lever bouncing afterwards.

88 Nerves and Muscles

Once the stimulus passes the threshhold, each muscle fibre gives an 'all or nothing' response to it. For the whole muscle, made up of many fibres, once the stimulus passes the threshhold, the small response gets bigger as more fibres reach their threshhold and contract. This happens progressively until the stimulus reaches its **maximal** value, which is not increased if the stimulus is made supramaximal. If two electrical impulses are applied, with only a short interval between them, the muscle responds with two contractions. But if the second stimulus is applied during the contraction phase produced by the first impulse, **summation** occurs: the second contraction is superimposed on the first to give a height on the tracing greater than that produced by a single impulse. When a rapid series of stimuli is applied a sustained contraction or **tetanus** occurs in the muscle. Tetanus lasts as long as the stimuli continue, or until fatigue comes on. Rates of stimulation just too low to give tetanus produce an **incomplete tetanus** or **clonus**. There is a very short period, called the **refractory period**, during which a second stimulus will not produce a second impulse. It is coincident in time with the action potential.

2 Fig. 51 is a diagram of tracings to illustrate these points. Match the list below to a tracing or to a part of a tracing in Fig. 51.

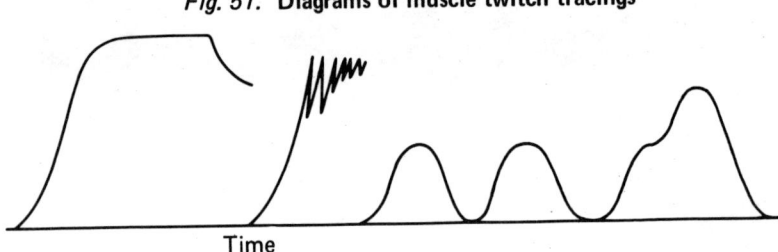

Fig. 51. **Diagrams of muscle twitch tracings**

a Response to one electrical impulse
b Response to two showing summation
c Response to two impulses with time between for complete muscle relaxation
d Tetanus
e Fatigue after tetanus
f Clonus

The amount of time a twitch takes can depend on the temperature. Fig. 52 is a diagram of two tracings for the same frog muscle, but one was done at 10 °C, and the other at 0 °C.

3 Say which is the tracing at 10 °C, and give the reason for your answer.

Fig. 52. **Muscle twitches at two temperatures**

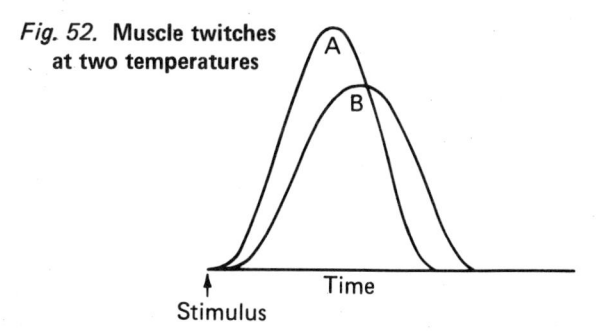

7.3 Neuromuscular transmission

A motor nerve ends on the surface of a muscle fibre in an end plate. When an impulse reaches the end plate an action potential similar to that in the nerve itself arises around the end plate and propagates in both directions along the muscle fibre. The muscle action potential is not set off by the electrical stimulus supplied by the nerve, as this stimulus is not strong enough to depolarise the very much larger area of the cell membrane of the muscle fibre. Instead, the impulse is carried across from nerve to muscle chemically, the muscle fibre membrane responding to the chemical (acetylcholine) released at the end plates by a large and immediate increase in permeability to sodium and potassium ions. This depolarisation has the same action as an electrical stimulus would give to the muscle.

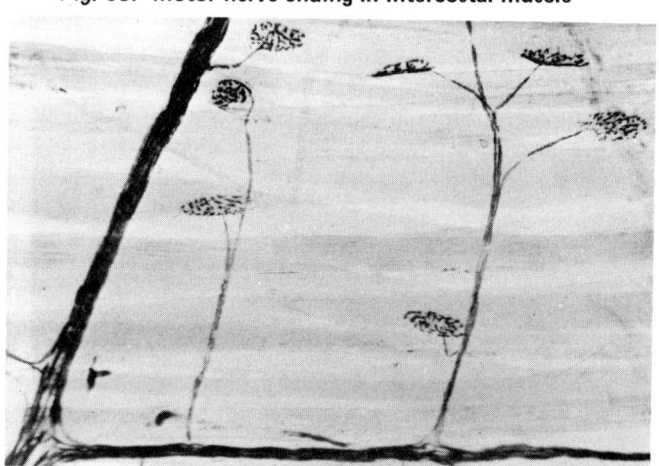

Fig. 53. **Motor nerve ending in intercostal muscle**

(Photograph by John Haller, Harris Biological Supplies)

90 Nerves and Muscles

Which of the following pieces of evidence **A** to **E** support the following two statements?

1 The nerve fibre excites the muscle chemically in some way.
2 It is at the nerve end plate that the chemical substance passes from the nerve to the muscle fibre.

A Dilute nicotine solution applied to the end plate region, but not when applied to the nerve or muscle alone, causes prolonged muscle twitching.

B Adrenaline, injected into the blood, causes many of the effects also caused by stimulation of sympathetic nerves: for example, increase of heart beat, rise in blood pressure.

C Fluid from a beating isolated frog's heart which has been slowed by stimulating the vagus nerve to it will cause the slowing of a second heart.

D The fatal South American arrow poison, curare, which causes paralysis of striated muscle, thus stopping breathing, can be used on a nerve-muscle preparation. After curare is applied generally to the preparation, the muscle does not contract when the nerve is stimulated, but it does if the stimulus is given directly to the muscle instead of to the nerve. If curare is put *only* on the nerve, the muscle contracts as usual when the nerve is stimulated.

E Acetylcholine delivered by a micropipette as close as possible to a motor end plate sets up a muscle impulse. It does not do so if it is delivered into the inside of the muscle fibre.

7.4 Reflexes

Reactions which seem to be automatic and immediate are called reflexes or reflex actions. Shining a light into the eye causes the pupil to constrict; touching the back of the throat causes a choking action; one blinks if something touches the cornea; a leg jerks when it is tapped smartly under the knee. These are all examples of reflex actions.

Originally the word 'reflex' implied that the message coming in via the sensory nerve was 'reflected' in the central nervous system and out into the motor nerve which then caused a muscle to react. As early as 1730 Stephen Hales, rector at Teddington, Middlesex, showed that it was likely that the nervous pathway from the skin of the foot went through the spinal cord and out to the leg muscles. Using a frog which had had its head cut off, he pinched one foot. The leg was drawn up away from the stimulus. The withdrawal action did not happen when the spinal cord was destroyed.

At the beginning of the nineteenth century Magendie and Bell carried this work further. Here is a summary of their experiments:

Each spinal nerve splits into two branches close to the spinal cord. One branch, the dorsal root, joins the cord dorsally, and the other — the ventral root — joins it ventrally.

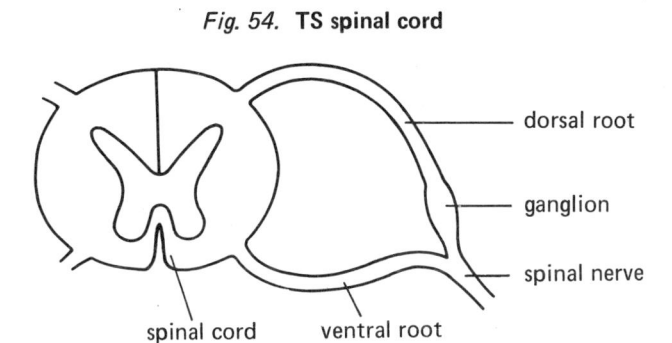

Fig. 54. **TS spinal cord**

- dorsal root
- ganglion
- spinal nerve
- spinal cord
- ventral root

After the ventral root was cut through, exciting that part of the nerve going to the body caused muscular contraction, but no signs of sensation. Exciting the part still attached to the spinal cord did not cause contraction, neither did the animal show any signs of sensation. When the *dorsal* root was cut through, nearly the reverse happened. The part of the nerve going to the body caused no muscular movement or sensation, whereas the part attached to the cord caused pain and also produced movement.

1 How did these experiments show that the ventral roots are exclusively motor with no sensory function, and that the dorsal roots are exclusively sensory but can cause movement by 'reflection' in the spinal cord?

Conditioned reflex

The initial work on conditioned reflexes was done by the Russian physiologist, Pavlov, at the turn of this century. Dogs were trained to stand still in a quiet room, their movement restricted only by loops passing loosely round the legs. In Pavlov's experiments food in the mouth is the unconditioned reflex for the production of saliva. He established that the sight and smell of food also caused salivation, and this he called a conditioned response. His experiments involved the giving of another stimulus such as the ticking of a metronome or the sound of a tuning fork at, or close to, the time when food was presented. Results from one experiment with one dog are given in the table on page 92. A note was sounded for five seconds, and food was given after a further two or three seconds. To test the strength of the new reflex the note was then sounded for 30 seconds and the drops of saliva produced during this period counted. There are many other experiments which have given rise to a considerable amount of literature on the subject.

Number of times that food and sound were given together	Then: Drops of saliva produced in 30 seconds when the sound was given alone	Number of seconds between the sound when given alone and the production of saliva
1	0	—
10	6	18
20	20	8
30	60	2
40	62	1
50	59	2

2 How has the reflex action been modified?

Some of the experiments used two similar stimuli, only one of which was followed by food, and it was, for example, established that a dog can distinguish between different shapes and degrees of luminosity, but it cannot distinguish colours if their luminosity is equal.

One result of some of these experiments was a 'neurotic' dog. When an experiment involved fine and difficult discriminations the animal showed signs of stress, becoming excitable and bad-tempered, although it could be restored to normal after long treatment.

3 Do you think it is possible to extrapolate from this to the way in which strain and fatigue can be caused in man?

7.5 Muscle contraction

Striated muscle, also called voluntary muscle, makes up those muscles of the body which can be controlled by the person. The basic unit of striated muscle is the fibre, which may be as long as the muscle. Each fibre is made up of many myofibrils which run from end to end of the fibre. Each myofibril has light and dark bands across it which lie next to those of the other myofibrils so that the whole fibre appears banded. It is with the structure and action of the bands that this problem is concerned. The arrangement of the bands, as revealed by the electron microscope, is shown in Fig. 55 and, diagrammatically, in Fig. 56.

The bands, which are repeated all along the length of the myofibril, have a repeating unit called the sarcomere which begins and ends at a dark line called the Z line, and which is between 2.0 µm and 3.5 µm long. Lying centrally between two Z lines is the wide A band, in the middle of which is

Nerves and Muscles 93

Fig. 55. EM of striated muscle of rat to show detail of sarcomere. A, I and H bands, and Z line, are marked. g: glycogen granules.

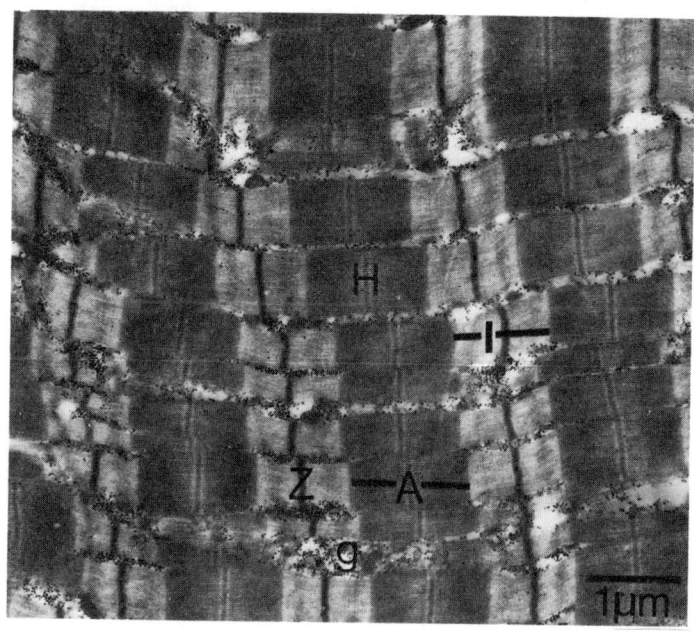

(Photograph by J.H. Kugler, from transparency set EMI, Harris Biological Supplies)

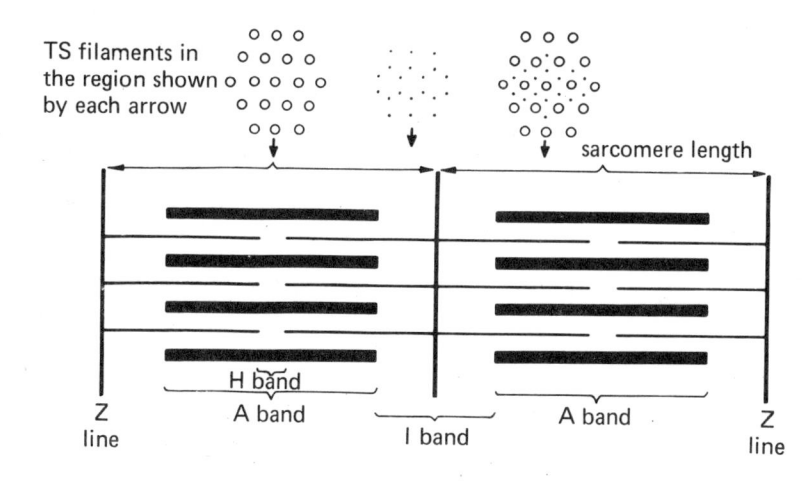

Fig. 56. Diagrammatic section through mammalian striated muscle

the H band. The area between two A bands, which has the Z line through its centre, is the I band. At higher magnification the A band is seen to contain rod-like, fairly thick filaments (11 nm). The I bands contain thinner filaments (4 nm), which extend into the A band area between the thick filaments. These thick and thin filaments are arranged in a particular way, as shown by the cross-sectional diagrams in Fig. 56. The myofibril therefore is made up of two sets of overlapping, interpenetrating filaments.

Two proteins, myosin and actin, are obtained from muscle. The myosin constitutes about 35 per cent of the total protein in muscle, the actin about 15 per cent. Using suitable solutions it is possible to extract each of these proteins from muscle. It is found that myosin occurs only in the A bands, whereas actin occurs in the I bands and in the outer parts of the A bands. Actin does not occur in the H band.

1 What does this evidence suggest that each type of filament is made of?

These two proteins, extracted from muscle, can be spun into filaments. When ATP is added, such filaments contract and can even lift weights.

2 Does this evidence suggest that the filaments could be the contractile unit of the muscle?

When the myofibril contracts, or is stretched by the experimenter, some of the bands change in length. The filaments are not disorientated during contraction: they do not coil, kink or fold up.

Fig. 57 shows diagrammatically the changes which occur.

Fig. 57. **Contracted and stretched striated muscle. Diagram to show the position of thick and thin filaments**

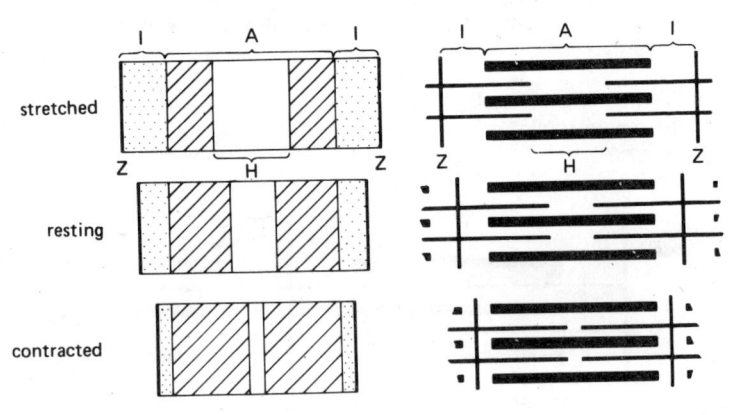

3 As the muscle contracts and gets shorter, what happens to the A, H and I bands: do they get longer, shorter or remain the same?

Nerves and Muscles 95

4 The filaments do not coil, kink or fold up during contraction, neither are they disorientated in any way. Suggest how the changes in band size noted in your answer to question 3 could happen.

Each thick filament has side chains sticking out from the thick filaments to the six neighbouring thin filaments. From one side chain to another is about five per cent of the length of half the sarcomere, but muscle can shorten by about 30 per cent. The sliding filament theory of contraction proposes that the force of contraction is developed in the region where two sets of filaments overlap. Shortening could be caused by links forming between the side chains and the thin filaments, the side chains moving forwards, breaking the link, forming another and moving again, thus causing one filament to slide or climb up the other.

5 How many times must one link detach from one site on a thin filament and re-attach to another to account for a shortening of 30 per cent?

7.6 Glycolysis in muscle

The facts listed below as 1 to 5 were gathered during the early experimental work on the contraction of muscles. Say which of the facts 1 to 5 support, even if they do not offer direct evidence for, each of the statements A to E.

1 A muscle uses oxygen and produces carbon dioxide, the intake and production of which increase if the muscle is contracting. Glycogen is used up.

2 A muscle will contract in the absence of oxygen but unlike a muscle supplied with oxygen, will not recover during a rest period and then contract again. In anaerobic conditions the glycogen disappears, and lactic acid is formed, in proportion to each other.

3 Lactic acid is produced during contraction but only in small amounts unless muscular activity is very vigorous. More accumulates in the absence of oxygen but the muscle stops contracting; when oxygen is supplied to this muscle it is able to contract again and the lactic acid disappears.

4 A muscle treated with iodoacetate (a poison) can contract for a time without the production of lactic acid but contraction stops sooner than under normal anaerobic conditions. Glycogen disappears as before.

5 If a person has a spurt of activity which needs more oxygen than the lungs can provide during the time the activity is going on, an oxygen debt develops. Also lactic acid accumulates in the muscles. The person will breathe quickly and deeply for some time after the exercise.

A Oxygen is not necessary for muscle contraction, but is necessary for muscle recovery after contraction.

96 Nerves and Muscles

B The energy for contraction comes from the glycogen.
C Glycogen is converted to lactic acid under anaerobic conditions.
D There must be more than one reaction in the appearance of lactic acid from glycogen. Iodoacetate blocks the later reaction(s).
E Lactic acid is removed by the action of oxygen.

7.7 Rods and cones

The retina of the human eye contains the visual receptor cells: the rods and cones. Their elongated processes synapse with the bipolar cells which in turn synapse with the ganglion cells. The axons of the ganglion cells converge to leave the eye at the blind spot as the optic nerve. Light has to pass through the ganglion cell and bipolar cell layers to reach the rods and cones.

Fig. 58. **Diagram to show the main synaptic connections in the retina**

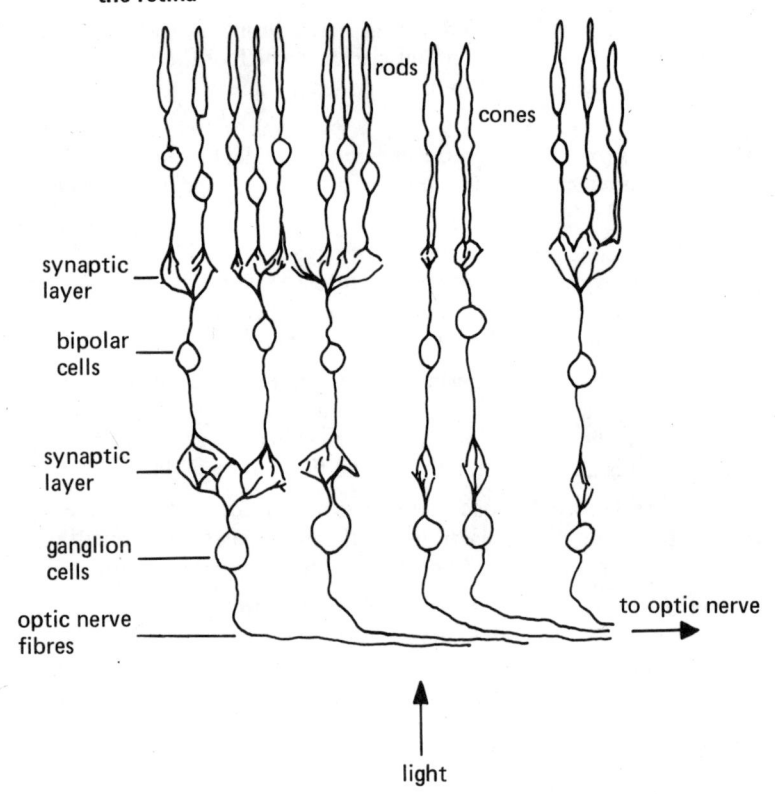

Nerves and Muscles 97

The *rods* are very sensitive to light, and are the receptors for night vision. There are about sixty-five million rods in each eye. Several rods are connected to each bipolar cell, and several bipolar cells to one ganglion cell.

The *cones* have a much higher threshold than the rods, can only work well in high light intensity and have a much greater accuracy. They can see colour and are responsible for vision in bright light. There are about three and a half million in each eye. A lot of the cones are connected singly to one bipolar cell and do not share the connection with other cones.

1 In the eye of nocturnal mammals would you expect there to be more rods or cones?

The visual acuity of the eye is the degree to which details are seen. It is visual acuity which is tested by the charts of different sized letters at the opticians. Fig. 59 (below) shows the relative acuity of vision in the central and peripheral areas of the human retina in a person who has been some time in a darkened room, and one in the light. Fig. 60 (page 98) shows the numbers of rods and cones across a human retina.

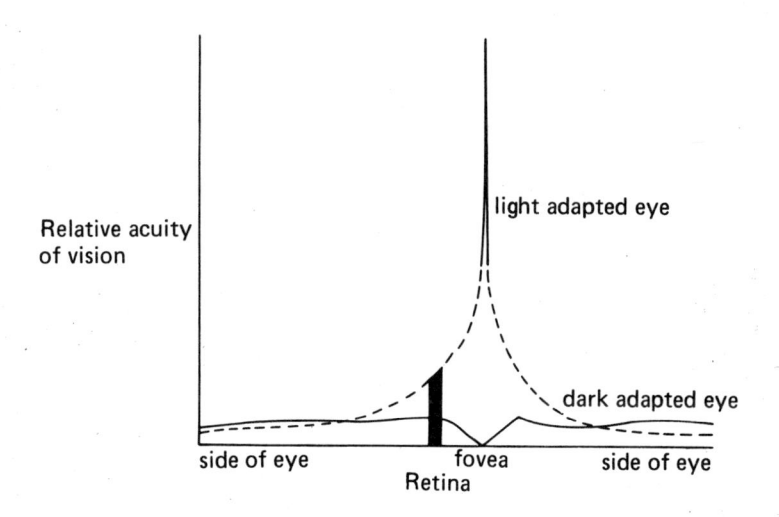

Fig. 59. **Relative acuity of vision in central and peripheral portions of the human retina**

2 What do you think the black area represents in Figs. 59 and 60?
3 How do Figs. 59 and 60 bear out the characteristics of rods and cones as described above?

Fig. 60. **Rod and cone density in central and peripheral portions of the human retina**

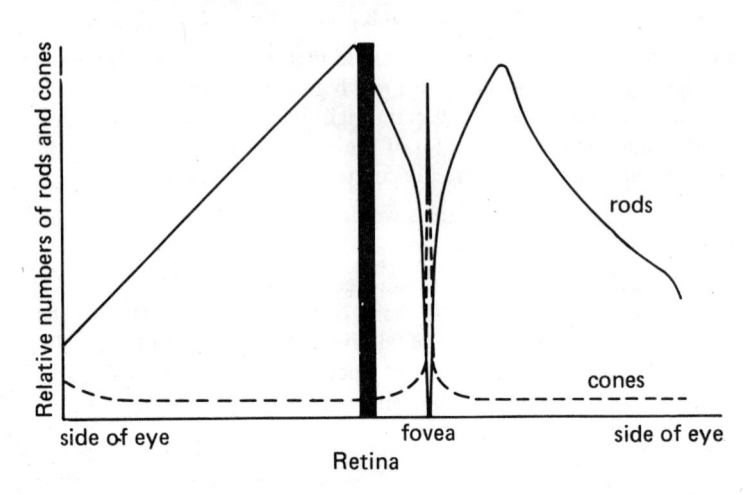

4 Compare the light- and dark-adapted eyes. Which eye sees more clearly
   a with the central part of the retina
   b with the peripheral portion of the retina?

5 The following two lists contain **A** observations about vision, and **B** details of rod and cone distribution and connections. Match one or more of the items in list **B** with each item in list **A**.

A

The peripheral parts of the retina
   i   are exceedingly sensitive to dim light
   ii   are colour blind
   iii appreciate movement at night very readily
   iv   have poor perception of detail, even in bright light.

The fovea centralis
   v   does not appreciate light of low intensity
   vi   sees colour
   vii is extremely acute in perceiving fine detail.
   viii Parts of the retina between the periphery and the fovea can perceive colour and also react, without colour vision, to light of low intensity. Such parts do not, however, appreciate fine detail as well as the fovea does.
   ix   You can see an object better in dim light if you look a little to one side of it rather than directly at it.

B

a The peripheral parts of the retina contain very many rods and few cones.
b The peripheral parts of the retina are also very receptive to light of short duration.
c In the peripheral parts of the retina a number of rods connect to each bipolar cell and there may be several bipolar cells to each ganglion cell.
d There are cones only in the fovea centralis.
e Cones have a high threshold of stimulation.
f The cones in the fovea are very closely packed and each cone is connected to its own nerve fibre to the brain.
g The retina between the periphery and the fovea contains both rods and cones.

Red light stimulates the rods only a little but allows the cones to function well. Radiologists, aircraft pilots and others who need good visual sensitivity in dim light can become dark-adapted by spending twenty minutes in the dark before working in dim light. Alternatively, and less boringly, they can wear red goggles when in bright light and then go direct to the dimly lit area.

6 Explain how the eyes become adapted by wearing the goggles.

Problems in Animal Physiology
TEACHERS' NOTES

1 Gas Exchange and Respiration

1.1 Lung capacity

1 1 Vital capacity.
  2 Residual volume.
  3 Inspiratory reserve volume.
  4 Expiratory reserve volume.
  5 Tidal volume.

2 a 4.8 dm^3 b 3.1 dm^3

3 a 6.0 dm^3 b 4.2 dm^3

4 a 11 and 13.
  b 1.4 dm^3 and 2.3 dm^3

5 Breathing is faster and deeper.

6 The oxygen in the cylinder is being used up as the subject breathes and the carbon dioxide he produces is being absorbed, so the spirometer bell falls.

7 Carbon dioxide should be absorbed efficiently as excess will soon lead to respiratory distress. There should be very little dead space or breathing becomes laboured. Dead space is that part of the respiratory system which is not available for gas exchange, that is, all except the alveoli. A long snorkel or, in the case of a spirometer, a long tube between the oxygen in the cylinder and the mouth, becomes an extension of the dead space. For each cm^3 of tube volume, the depth of inspiration would have to be increased by 1 cm^3 to supply the same volume of air to the alveoli.

1.2 Control of breathing

1 Both rate and depth of breathing increase.

2 At least in the early part of the investigation the excess carbon dioxide is exhaled in the faster and deeper breathing movements.

3 During exercise, or if the level of carbon dioxide in an enclosed space rises.

Gas Exchange and Respiration 103

4 Carbon dioxide. When the percentage of carbon dioxide in the alveoli increases, there is a rise in the amount of carbon dioxide in the blood. This affects the respiratory centre in the brain which in turn, by nervous control, causes changes in breathing.

1.3 Adaptations to high altitude

1 Increased number of red blood cells, increased output of blood from the heart, haemoglobin which will load with oxygen more readily than that of sea level dwellers, giving a dissociation curve to the left of normal.

2 For each species the number of red blood cells is higher at altitude than at sea level.

1.4 Diving mammals

During a dive:

With the peripheral circulation almost shut off, and oxygen demand reduced, the heart pumps blood round a much reduced circuit. The heart rate can be reduced and yet the same amount of blood as normal can be circulated.

The muscles, shut off from the oxygen supply in the blood, use up the myoglobin oxygen, and then respire anaerobically with the rapid accumulation of lactic acid, which cannot yet be removed by the blood as it is not circulating through the muscle. The lactic acid content of the blood thus remains at or near normal.

After a dive:

The lactic acid is removed from the muscles by the blood now circulating at the normal rate, and the oxygen debt is repaid.

1.5 Measurement of metabolic rate

1 a A decrease in dry mass would indicate loss of respiratory substrate, but would mean sacrificing the organism to find its dry mass. A population would therefore need to be sampled at intervals. Changes in fresh mass need not be due to respiration but could, for example, be caused by gain or loss of water.

 b Uptake of oxygen can be measured using a respirometer or Warburg unit. It is technically easy and gives good results.

 c Using the amount of food eaten is cumbersome and could be inaccurate. Metabolism continues using stored materials even if the animal eats nothing for some time. On the other hand it could be eating in excess of requirements and storing the excess as fat. Food itself contains varying amounts of water. In addition, food is used for growth as

104 Gas Exchange and Respiration

well as respiration.

d A fairly crude indication of heat production is given by using a thermometer. A better way is to use an electrical device held in the tissues under carefully controlled conditions.

2 The body may contain an unknown amount of water, and varying amounts of slowly respiring tissues such as bone and fat. Uptake of oxygen will vary considerably with activity. It isn't easy to measure the BMR of animals other than man, as there will probably be difficulty in getting a true basal resting state.

3 Possibly:
   mouse — oxygen consumption, loss of mass
   elephant — food intake
   fish — food intake, oxygen consumption
   plant — in the dark, oxygen consumption, carbon dioxide production
   seeds — in the dark, oxygen consumption, carbon dioxide, heat production.

1.6 Calculation of basal metabolic rate

1 The man uses 300 cm^3 oxygen per minute
= 300 x 60 = 18 dm^3 oxygen per hour.
$\therefore$ BMR = $\frac{18 \times 20.17}{1.9}$ = 191.1 kJ m^{-2} h^{-1}

2 During 24 hours he would expend 191.1 x 24 kJ m^{-2}
So he needs to eat 191.1 x 24 x 1.9 kJ food
= 8714 kJ.

1.7 Metabolic rate and size

2 As body mass decreases, metabolic rate increases.

3 The smaller the mammal the greater the surface area per gram, the greater the heat loss, and therefore the higher the cost of temperature regulation.

4 In the table there is a much more constant relationship between heat produced and surface area. If metabolic rate is expressed instead in terms of body mass then there are marked differences between animals of different masses.

5 The reptile is a poikilotherm, and is not involved in maintaining a constant body temperature.

6 As size decreases, metabolic rate increases and finding and processing enough food would become impossible. A man eats about one-fortieth of his body mass per day. A shrew eats its total body mass per day.

Gas Exchange and Respiration 105

7 Support: as mass increases in three dimensions, leg cross-sectional area increases only in two. Compare the mass of marine mammals supported by the water. A whale can weigh considerably more than an elephant.

8 The elephant would not be able to get enough food. It would also not be able to lose the heat produced.

1.8 Oxygen consumption and activity

1 Comparing related organisms (the octopus which moves along the sea bed with the squid which swims, the slow eel with the much faster trout) there is a greater uptake in the more active animal. And a very active animal (such as the humming bird) has a high uptake even when at rest.

2 Mouse.

3 Mouse. It needs more oxygen per gram than man does.

4 The metabolic rate is higher in the early years and during adolescence. Growth, the synthesis of body constituents, is an energy-consuming process. When growth stops the basal metabolism levels out, and as a person ages it starts to decline.

1.9 Oxygen consumption and temperature

1 The homoiotherm, which would have a body temperature considerably above that of the poikilotherm.

2 The low metabolic rate of poikilotherms at low temperatures restricts their activity. They must be sufficiently active to get enough food, so a geographical limit to their spread is set by temperature.

3 At lower temperatures the homoiotherms generate more heat which maintains normal body temperature. Their oxygen consumption increases as metabolic energy is spent in heat production.

4 The heat given off would increase as the mouse uses more energy to regulate its temperature by shivering.

5 a There is a considerable fall in metabolic rate during hibernation, the heart and breathing rate slow right down.
  b There is not enough food available in the cold season.

1.10 Oxygen consumption in water

1 a The volume of oxygen dissolved in the water decreases as the temperature rises.
  b The volume of oxygen needed by the fish increases with rising temperature.

106 Gas Exchange and Respiration

2 The problem is how to get ever increasing amounts of oxygen from an ever decreasing oxygen supply.

3 The rate of ventilation increases.

4 The fish will be in real difficulties when the amount of oxygen obtained by increased ventilation is completely used in providing the energy for the increased ventilation.

5 Like the fish, the snail needs an increasing volume of oxygen as the temperature rises. There is little increase in oxygen uptake between 5 °C and 15 °C, then up to 30 °C the Q_{10} is about 2.

1.11 Respiratory quotient

1 Man. Mixed fat and carbohydrate.
Earthworm. Mainly fat.
Drosophila, at rest. Conversion of carbohydrate to fat during the rest period.
Drosophila, during flight. Carbohydrate.
Nerve tissue. Mainly fat.
Brain. Mainly carbohydrate.
Geese, forced feeding. Conversion of carbohydrate to fat during the fattening process.
Geese, basal diet. Mainly fat.
Paramecium. Mainly carbohydrate.

2 Changes in RQ can be caused by changes in diet at different developmental stages. The RQ is also, as in the geese figures, dependent on the food available to the animal.

3 During exercise the RQ rises because carbon dioxide is being blown off while an oxygen debt is being contracted. After exercise, more oxygen is taken in and the oxygen debt cleared.

2 Blood System

2.1 Origin of heart beat

1 They indicate that the heart can contract without stimulation by nerves, that is, that the heart beat is myogenic (a property of the muscle itself) and not neurogenic (due to nervous stimulation).
2 The muscle.
3 Yes. It seems that the sequence of contraction in the heart is determined by the part which has the highest degree of spontaneous activity. An impulse which starts in the sino-atrial node excites the whole heart as it is conducted over it.
4 When the Purkinje fibres are cut the heart beat changes or stops.

2.2 Blood vessels

1 The capillaries have a total cross-sectional area about 1000 times greater than that of the aorta. Although very narrow there are many of them. The diameter of the lumens of veins and vena cavae is greater than that of the arteries and aorta, and there are some differences in wall thickness connected with the amount of muscle in, and contractile power of, arteries as compared with veins.
2 The percentages given in the table do not add up to 100 per cent. Eight per cent of the blood is in pulmonary circulation, and the rest is in the heart. The total cross-sectional area of the venous system is much greater than that of the arterial system. Since there is approximately an equal length of vessels in each, the total volume will be greater in the venous system. Flow in the arterial system is phasic because of the heart beat, some vessels will be contracted.
3 Aorta, vein, venule, capillary.
4 Pressure will be highest in the aorta, lowest in the vena cava (see graph). It drops from 120 mmHg in the aorta to 5 mmHg in the vena cava.
5 A: mean velocity
  B: mean pressure
  C: total cross-sectional area.

108 Blood System

2.3 Capillary circulation

1   a 32 - 8 = .24 mmHg.
    b 12 - 8 = 4 mmHg.
2   25 - 10 = 15 mmHg.
3   a 24 - 15 = 9 mmHg.
    b 4 - 15 = -11 mmHg.
4   Fluid will be forced out at the arteriole end and drawn in at the venule end of the capillary. In fact, the amount of fluid moving out of capillaries normally exceeds that moving in, which would eventually stop completely the filtration described above. However, extra fluid moving out enters the blind ending lymphatic capillaries and finally enters the blood system as lymph through veins in the neck.
5   With little protein in the diet there are fewer proteins in the blood, the effective OP of the plasma will fall, and the effective filtration pressure at both ends of the capillary will rise. More fluid is forced out at the arteriole end, and less drawn in at the venule end.

2.4 Foetal circulation in man

2   It is diverted through the ductus arteriosus to the aorta.
3   The foramen ovale between the right and left atria allows oxygenated blood to get to the aorta, as does the ductus arteriosus.
4   Blood returning from the newly used lungs after birth causes the pressure in the left atrium to rise, pushing the valve of the foramen ovale to close the hole. A few minutes after birth the ductus arteriosus constricts, and closes a few hours later. After a few days of life both holes have fused shut and the adult circulation is established. If the foramen ovale or ductus arteriosus do not fully close, some deoxygenated blood will enter the aorta and tissues will not get fully oxygenated arterial blood. This can cause cyanosis, weakness, poor growth, and even mental retardation.

2.5 Blood pigments

1   Haemoglobin and chlorocruorin are very similar, then haemoglobin, then haemerythrin.
2   Vastly. Sea water itself carries only about 0.5 cm^3 oxygen in 100 cm^3 water. One would expect an animal having a body fluid with no respiratory pigment to be a fairly sluggish creature.

3 Vertebrate haemoglobin is carried in cells, which are packed with haemoglobin to give a high concentration. It seems that a more efficient blood as far as oxygen carriage is concerned contains a respiratory pigment, haemoglobin, packed in cells.

2.6 Oxygen carriage

1 There is rapid loading in the lungs. The amount of oxygen in the air can vary widely while still giving very nearly full saturation of the haemoglobin. On the other hand in the tissues, where there is a low partial pressure of oxygen, there is rapid unloading.

2 For all, dissociation becomes more rapid with the increase.

3 Exercise means a faster use of oxygen, and a lower partial pressure, which can approach zero in exercising muscle, is reached. More heat and carbon dioxide are generated than at rest, and there is a slight increase in acidity. All these changes make more oxygen available.

4 $(19.79 - 15.22) \times 45 = 205.65 \text{ cm}^3$ oxygen.

5 Foetal haemoglobin has a greater affinity for oxygen. It will therefore take oxygen from the mother's blood across the placenta.

2.7 Dissociation curves

Man breathes air which has a high oxygen availability. The mackerel lives in an environment where oxygen is not very soluble. It is, however, a pelagic fish swimming almost continuously in the upper, relatively well oxygenated, waters.

Arenicola leads a slow life in the sand with oxygen-poor water around it except when the tide is out during which time its water is not replenished.

The haemoglobin of the mackerel reaches a high saturation at lower partial pressures of oxygen than that of man; *Arenicola* at very much lower partial pressures. For example, at a pO_2 of 10 mmHg the haemoglobin of man is only 15 per cent saturated, mackerel is 25 to 30 per cent, and *Arenicola* is 90 per cent. It seems that the haemoglobin of each suits the environment in which each lives.

2.8 The transport of carbon dioxide

1 Venous, as the column is shown between tissues and lungs.
2 Plasma.

110 Blood System

3 a As the hydrogen carbonate ion. **b** Dissolved.

The figures are: carbon dioxide in solution   5 to 10 per cent
carbamino compounds   10 to 20 per cent
bicarbonate ions   70 to 80 per cent.

4 It is discharged in the lungs.

5 4.5 dm³ blood going round the body once excrete 45 x 5 = 225 cm³ carbon dioxide per minute.

2.9 Blood groups

1 The plasma of blood group O has both antibodies; B has anti-A.

2 a Nothing.
  b Agglutination.

3 a

A donor with blood group	A	B	AB	O
can give blood to	A,AB	B,AB	AB	all 4

b

A patient with blood group	A	B	AB	O
can receive blood from	A,O	B,O	A,B,AB,O	O

4 a Group O.
  b Group AB.

2.10 Inheritance of blood groups

1 a O   **b** A, B.

2 A, B.

3 AO and BO.

4 A person with a blood group of AB could not have produced one with a blood group of O, but someone with a genotype AO could have done.

3 Growth and Reproduction

3.1 Growth in humans

1. There are two growth spurts. One is in infancy and is partly a continuation of the foetal growth period. The second is at puberty, just before growth stops.
2. Height. Changes in mass may be due to fat deposition, or a person may get slimmer. In addition the amount of water in the body varies.
3. Height and most body measurements follow the general curve. The reproductive curve is slow until puberty and then very rapid. The brain and skull develop earlier than any other part of the body.
4. For the mouse puberty rapidly follows weaning, and the greatest rate of growth is just after birth. There is no adolescent spurt because there is no period of reduced growth rate between birth and maturity.
5. The main difference between the growth pattern of a primate and that of other mammals is the postponement of puberty in primates. Between weaning and puberty, with its adolescent growth spurt, the primate brain grows and matures (see Fig. 19). This period may be an evolutionary feature associated with the primates. It is probably advantageous for learning and may be good for patterns of social life. The young are still sexually immature and although they can take part in group life they can still be dominated and do not challenge the adults.
6. Males are bigger on average than females at maturity, but girls mature about two years earlier than boys. Changes in physiological function also occur at adolescence, and are much more marked in boys than girls. After adolescence, boys are stronger, their hearts and lungs are larger relative to their size, they have a greater oxygen-carrying capacity, and a greater power to absorb lactic acid and other substances produced by muscles. The male's athletic ability therefore increases greatly at adolescence. Other sex differences in growth include:

 Girls are generally about four weeks ahead of boys in skeletal maturity at birth. From then to adulthood boys stay at about 80 per cent of the skeletal age of girls of the same age.

 Boys have wider shoulders, and girls wider hips, largely due to the stimulation of cartilage cells by sex hormones.

112 Growth and Reproduction

A boy's legs are longer relative to his trunk because of a longer period of prepubescent growth when the legs are growing faster than the trunk.

By birth, a boy's forearm is longer relative to the upper arm, and this increases gradually during the whole growing period.

The first finger is longer than the third more often in girls than boys.

At puberty a boy's face changes more than a girl's. The jaw becomes longer, also thicker and it thus projects more, the profile becomes straighter the nose more projecting, and the incisors of both jaws are more upright.

3.2 Thyroid action

1 Hyperthyroidism. Raised temperature, insensitivity to cold, flushed skin, high pulse and loss of mass can be attributed to thyroxine acting on the metabolic rate. Mass is lost because of increased catabolism of tissue protein and oxidation of stored fat. The eyes protrude because of a cushion of fat behind them (not caused by excess thyroxine). Any goitre present is caused by the enlargement of the thyroid, the enlargement resulting in the production of the excess thyroxine.

Hypothyroidism: myxoedema. Symptoms showing a lowered metabolic rate are the slowing of processes, a low body temperature and poor resistance to cold. The characteristic puffiness is caused by protein-carbohydrate compounds accumulating under the skin and retaining water.

In a child dwarfism is caused by lack of thyroxine acting as a growth hormone. Incomplete myelination of nervous tissue causes mental retardation.

2 Mass decreases as the proteinaceous compounds and the retained water are removed after thyroxine has been given. The BMR is raised as would be expected and the pulse rate goes up. Both BMR and pulse rate decrease when the thyroxine dosage is stopped.

3 a myxoedema   b normal   c hyperthyroidism.

4 The overactive thyroid will take up a lot of iodine quickly and little will be excreted. The underactive thyroid takes up only a small amount of iodine, takes it up slowly, and a lot is excreted.

3.3 Nature and nurture

This is a long problem, dealing with material not usually tackled in a biology course. The background may be unfamiliar to students who may have personal points of view, and it probably lends itself better to discussion than to written answers. In addition it is a highly contentious area. Jensen's paper (table, page 35) and his analyses have received much criticism as well as support. It would be sensible to review the evidence and discussion before starting.

1 The children of eminent men have greater opportunities for the same kind of experiences which made their fathers famous. They have more influence acting for them in high places, and they live in houses with many books, and with interest and enthusiasm around them. It isn't surprising that they have the chance to do well.

What about the women? Why did they not inherit the scientific bent? Perhaps their environment prevented any scientific interest, ability or public recognition from appearing. Galton states that he would have been able to produce the names of women whose abilities were highly appreciated in private life, but felt that to do so was not consistent with decorum.

2 Intelligence, like stature, is probably controlled by a large number of genes. There is evidence to show that feeble-minded people have fewer neurones than normal people, with comparatively few branches from them, and that these are arranged in a less systematic way. A condition passed on by a single gene is phenylketonuria. Severe mental retardation arises because of the inability of the body to manufacture the enzyme phenylalanine hydroxylase. As a result phenylalanine and phenylpyruvic acid accumulate and, in a manner unknown, cause retardation.

3 A study of the actual correlations shows that, in general, they seem to differ from the theoretical value by an amount which could be attributed to the environment. Thus there is a difference between monozygotic twins reared apart and together, the former showing the lower correlation. There is a similar difference between sibs brought up apart and together. Foster parent and child show a slight positive correlation. Is this because foster children are often not chosen at random, but to match the prospective parents?

4 Three of the four correlations are higher for identical twins than for non-identical twins, and twins reared apart show lower correlations than twins together. Mass shows lower correlations than height for identical twins, especially in those reared apart where diet may have been very different. It seems that mass could be less heritable and more affected by the environment than height.

5 Helen's education and stimulating environment could have contributed to her higher scores. Gladys suffered on both counts.

6 Again, the contributory factors seem to lie in the unfavourable environment, coupled with lack of schooling, slightly less apparent in the gipsy children.

7 There is a wealth of discussion points here, and a large number of books for background reading. A useful one to start with is *The home and the school* by J.W.B. Douglas, available in a Panther edition.

Briefly, possible points are:

a Family size

If children were progressively less intelligent the later they were born into a family, their scores would give a low mean score to a large family. But there is no evidence to support this, it is difficult to see any genetical reason for it, and see point **b** where the last born tend to do better than the intermediates. A provocative point would be to ask if it is perhaps mainly intelligent parents who limit their families. Or is it that children in large families may suffer more deficiencies of care in infancy and childhood? In particular, a mother with two or more children cannot give as much conversation to each as she could to only one. There is evidence to suggest that it is particularly in verbal tests that such children fare badly when compared with only children, and that in non-verbal tests the differences are less. The verbal effect is more noticeable in children who are born close together; when they are widely spaced, test scores are relatively high. This provides evidence that it is particularly in the understanding and use of words that children from large families are handicapped.

b Sibship position

Could there be a genetic explanation? It seems unlikely. Other points for consideration: do the first born get more adult stimulation, and are the younger children brought up to a certain extent by their elder sibs, listening more to childish prattle than to adult talk? On the other hand, do the eldest suffer more from parental inexperience, and have more time off school because of infectious deseases which the younger ones then get over before school starts? Do parents have different attitudes to children in different family positions: is more expected of the eldest, are the youngest spoilt and given more attention than intermediates? Do the youngest benefit more from the extra money there may be by the time they come along? Do differing sex attitudes account for the difference between eldest boys and eldest girls: are girls more coddled, expected to do more home duties, have less pressure to succeed?

c d e Social class, parental attitudes, home and school

What things may parents of a high income or occupational group offer their children which may not be so readily available to the children of an unskilled worker? There could be a high level of parental education, knowledge and understanding of the educational system and how it works, the ability to help children in at least their early years of schooling, smaller families, opportunities for acquiring an extensive vocabulary, more spacious housing facilities, a quiet room to work in, books, puzzles, educational toys, nursery schooling, money for trips, social visits, extra-curricular activities, games such as chess, outings to museums, concerts,

Growth and Reproduction 115

theatres, and so on. Could any, some, or all of these extras help a child to get on well at school, increase his attainment scores or affect his measured I.Q.?

3.4 Control of menstrual cycle

A is supported by **1a, 1b, 1c, 1d, 4.**
B is supported by **1c, 2a, 2b, 4.**
C is supported by **3, 2.**
D is supported by **3.**
E is supported by **1d, 4.**
F is supported by **5.**
G is supported by all.

3.5 Ovulation and temperature

1 In Fig. 28 ovulation is indicated in the first cycle on day 9-10 when the temperature starts to rise after its drop. In the second cycle ovulation and conception occurred on day 10-11. No period is due and the temperature stays up at the end of the cycle.

2 If the egg lives for twenty-four hours and the sperm for forty-eight hours there is a period of up to three days during which intercourse could result in pregnancy. For a woman with a completely regular cycle with periods always occurring twenty-eight days apart, the ripe egg may be released anywhere from the twelfth to the sixteenth day of the cycle. There is no way of predicting beforehand when this will be. As the sperms live for two days even the temperature drop just before ovulation may be too late an indicator. This regular woman should therefore avoid intercourse from day 10 (when live sperm could await the possible egg on day 12) to day 17 (when the egg may still be present and alive) inclusive. Once the temperature rise has occurred and the higher temperature has been recorded for three days, the unsafe period is over. Combining the rhythm method with temperature readings provides a more reliable means of contraception than using the rhythm method alone.

However, in the problem, we are dealing with a variable cycle of twenty-one to twenty-nine days. For the shortest cycle, deduct seven days from day 10 above, and for the longest add one day. This gives day 3 as the first possible unsafe day and day 18 as the last unsafe day. Some women (about 15 per cent) have such irregular cycles that if they used the rhythm method of contraception they would never make love. Neither can it be used immediately after childbirth when the first few cycles are usually irregular. The figure for pregnancies among users of the rhythm method is quite high, and has been given as 24 per cent, higher than for any other method of contraception except that which depends on using the douche. The high failure rate may not be due entirely to the method, although sperm may occasionally live longer than two days or there may be a sudden change in the cycle. There may also be carelessness in counting or difficulty in keeping records. There is also a suggestion that intercourse may cause the release of the ovum.

3.6 Gametogenesis

1 Oogenesis and spermatogenesis have similar stages, but only one egg develops from the meiotic division.
2 The male. XY inheritance.
3 The egg contains a little yolk, the sperm is motile.
4 Fertilisation restores the diploid number of chromosomes, and initiates development.

3.7 Artificial insemination

1 Many things could be examined: contamination, temperature effects, the nature of the diluting liquid, handling, differences between individual bulls.
2 There are two types of sperm, X and Y.
3 Breeding experiments with each fraction.
4 By the morning the sperms had settled with the Y sperms nearer the top of the tube.
5 In birds it is the female which is heterogametic.

3.8 Reproduction behaviour

1 a The large, shelled eggs of reptiles and birds where the young develop over a relatively long period of time outside the mother would have the most yolk.
  b Mammals, where the fertilised egg rapidly draws on the mother for food, have the least.
2 The frogs adopt a mating position, giving a much higher rate of fertilisation than in the fish.

Growth and Reproduction   117

3   A possible hypothesis might be that the eggs and young of partridges are far more exposed to predation, being in a nest on the ground, than those of a blackbird whose nest is in a tree. In fact, however, it is possible to find large clutches in species which have protected nests (tits, for example, lay 5-16 eggs), and vice versa.

4   The mammals produce fewer offspring which have a high rate of survival and a great deal of parental care.

5   The number which reach sexual maturity would balance the number of adults which die. Each reproducing pair would leave two offspring behind to reproduce.

3.9 Hatching and temperature

1   The lower the temperature the longer it takes to hatching, but for the three higher temperatures roughly an equal number of temperature/hour units are needed in that the figures given by multiplying temperature by hours are about the same. At 15 °C hatching takes a very much longer time, indicating that 15 °C is very much below the optimum.

2   The natural habitat of *Xenopus* is a warm country (Africa), whereas that of the trout is quite cool during the time trout are hatching.

Presumably the optimum temperature for the development of each species is an adaptation to its natural habitat.

3.10 Growth-controlling products in tadpoles

1   The larger tadpoles may be removing something from the water needed by the smaller tadpoles, specifically there may be competition for food. There may also be overcrowding and lack of space.

2   There are many possible answers.

3   The research biologists who did this work took culture water in which large tadpoles had been growing well and reused it as culture water for a small number of tadpoles which had just begun to feed. Their growth was inhibited.

In addition, they found that the inhibitor was removed by heating the water to 60 °C, centrifugation and filtration.

Growth and Reproduction
3.11 Metamorphosis in frogs
The evidence which supports each conclusion is given below:
A: 1, 2, 3, 4, 5, 11, 12.
B: 3, 5, 12.
C: 6, 7.
D: 7.
E: 7, 8, 9, 10.
F: 7, 8, 9.
G: 8, 9, 10.
H: 3, 5, 11, 12.
I: 5, 12.

3.12 Litter size and survival
1 Taking the six-week curve, twelve is the optimum size.
2 The larger the litter, the higher the mortality. The date when results are taken is important; even six weeks may be too early to judge the optimum size.
3 In wild pigs fewer would survive.
4 Two.

4 Excretion

4.1 Urea production and excretion

When the kidneys are removed first (1 and 2) there is an immediate rise in blood urea, indicating that urea is no longer being excreted by the kidneys but is still being made by the liver. After removal of the liver, the curve remains more or less steady, indicating that urea is neither being made nor excreted. This is seen also in 3. When only the liver is removed as in 4, blood urea falls as it is excreted by the kidneys.

4.2 Nitrogenous excretion in man

1 Water, urea, uric acid, creatinine, ammonia, sodium, potassium, calcium, magnesium, chloride, phosphate, sulphate.

2 Proteins, glucose.

3 It suggests that creatinine comes from the breakdown of tissues, and possibly by a different metabolic pathway.

4 It controls the pH of the blood.

4.3 Nitrogenous excretion in vertebrates

1 Aquatic organisms such as fish and tadpoles have access to a plentiful supply of water, and can excrete ammonia quickly and efficiently. Land animals, even the amphibians which return to the water for some of the time, cannot allow ammonia to accumulate. Urea is formed and remains in the animal's body for some time before being excreted.

Differences in the higher vertebrates are also correlated with their type of reproduction. The excretion of uric acid is associated with development inside an egg with an impermeable shell. Such eggs have a very limited water supply. Ammonia could not be disposed of, and the production of urea would upset the osmotic relationships of the cells and bind up a lot of the water supply. Instead, uric acid, which is both non-toxic and insoluble, accumulates during development. For the viviparous mammals, connected to the maternal blood stream, water supply is not such a problem, and urea can be excreted by the mother's kidneys. In terrestrial vertebrates the kind of nitrogenous excretion present in the embryo tends to persist when the animal becomes adult.

The evolutionary relationships of animals with similar or different nitrogenous end products, not discussed here, are worth exploring.

2   The aquatic species excrete about equal amounts of ammonia and urea. There is very little ammonia in those which do not live in water. The land species have a fair amount of urea but even more uric acid, and the desert species almost entirely uric acid.

3   a   Water is no longer available for the removal of ammonia, which must be cut down.

b and c   When water is removed urea is excreted as an alternative to ammonia, and is stored until the toad is back in water, when the excess urea is excreted over a period of days.

4.4   The kidney in bony fish

Accounts of kidney action in teleosts are given in sixth-form biology books, e.g. M.B.V. Roberts, *Biology. A Functional Approach*, Nelson, 1976, 2nd Ed, page 222.

4.5   Regulation of body fluids in four invertebrates

1   *Maia* lives in the sea and is unable to regulate the salt content of its tissue fluids, being always isotonic with the sea water in which it lives so that as the external water becomes more dilute so do its tissue fluids.

Estuarine waters change twice daily from sea water to fresh water, so estuarine animals must be able to withstand quite wide changes in the external medium.

Carcinus can regulate, to a certain degree, its internal fluid concentration as the water becomes more dilute. The tissues are not subject to wide fluctuation.

Nereis has a different mechanism from *Carcinus* to withstand the same changes: it has tissues which are able to work at both ends of the scale, although it does show a little more regulation than *Maia*.

2   Energy is required to regulate the internal body medium. As *Carcinus* moves to ever more dilute sea water, its oxygen consumption increases as more work is involved in regulating its internal environment. The figures for the two species of *Gammarus* could be used to support the same argument.

Excretion 121

4.6 Contractile vacuoles in protozoa

1 The contractile vacuole is osmoregulatory. It may also eliminate ions, but the data given shows no evidence for or against this.

2 Water can enter with the food in the food vacuole, through the gullet if there is one, and across the body surface. In *Amoeba mira*, no large vacuoles appear when the animal is not feeding.

3 i   opposes **a** because as the hydrostatic pressure difference between the vacuole and cytoplasm decreases as the vacuole fills up, one would expect the rate of inflow to slow down. It also opposes **b** as any solute inside the vacuole would be progressively diluted as the vacuole fills up, and the rate of osmotic inflow would slow down. If, however, solutes are being excreted into the vacuole at the same time as the water, this argument does not hold.

   ii opposes **a** as pressure in a shrunken cell is much lower than normal.

   iii and **iv** support **c**, implying an active metabolic mechanism involved in secretion across the vacuolar membrane.

5 Nutrition

5.1 Executives, alcohol and coffee

A Professional men in responsible positions are exposed more often than many other people to stress situations. Acid secretion in the stomach, under nervous control, is increased and ulcers may appear.

B With milk or oil lining the stomach the alcohol is held longer than if drinking is done on an empty stomach. It thus enters the intestine in a slow steady stream, and a sudden rise in blood alcohol with consequent intoxication is hopefully avoided.

C On the other hand, the beneficial effect of a moderate amount of alcohol or coffee is due to the stimulation of gastric secretions.

5.2 Diet and amylase activity

1 The secretion of salivary amylase is adapted to diet.
2 The amount of activity seems to show an adaptation to the diet of the people concerned, there being more activity with a diet of carbohydrates than with a carnivorous diet.
3 Exchange diets.
4 It suggests an adaptation to the prevailing diet, an adaptation which takes place relatively quickly, although the activity is still short of that of the other two groups.
5 A possible method would be to take a fixed amount of saliva under the same conditions and test the amount of digestion of a standard starch solution by colorimetry, or some other suitable way.

5.3 Energy requirements

1 **a, b** The number of kilojoules and the amount of protein required increase as a child grows, and reach their maxima during the adolescent spurt. Thereafter less is needed to maintain body mass and health. Girls peak at a lower age than boys as they reach puberty sooner. On average females need less than males. This is related to the difference in size.

Nutrition 123

c Pregnant and lactating women clearly need more food, and especially protein. However, during pregnancy a woman should not gain more than about 10 to 12 kg. Any extra gain is simply deposited as fat in her own body and may prove difficult to lose later.

2 The larger or more active a person, the more is needed. At lower temperatures more food is needed than at higher in order to maintain body temperature.

3 a Wealthy, technologically advanced.

b Poor food distribution, deficiencies at certain times of year due to catastrophes or insufficient stocks, climatic differences reflected in the amount of the harvest, lower social groups may show a degree of undernutrition not apparent elsewhere. Even in England and America some people suffer from malnutrition, often because of lack of knowledge of what constitutes a good diet. Some people say that obesity is a form of malnutrition.

c A large and expanding population, especially of young people, poor climate, poor land for agriculture, and so on. This is a discussion question, which could lead to implications and possible solutions.

d A person is hungry, obviously enough, because he does not eat enough food; he has a diet deficient in kilojoules. It is possible, however, for a person to eat a diet adequate in kilojoules and still be undernourished. Malnutrition is due to poor quality food and unbalanced diet, particularly one lacking in proteins. Kwashiorkor, common in the tropics, and especially severe in young children, is caused by a diet grossly deficient in animal protein. There is anaemia, a fatty enlarged liver, oedema and many other disturbances leading to death unless treated by eating protein. Other deficiency diseases attributable to malnutrition are common in such countries. (Kwashiorkor is also mentioned in problem 2.3).

5.4 Milk and diet

1 That milk contained some supplementary food factors, not present in the normal diet, which aided growth and prevented the illness and death of the animal.

2 Yes. But note that the rats without milk are gaining some mass for the first two weeks or so of their lives, but not as much as the rats with milk. Presumably they have a store of the 'supplementary food factors' in their bodies.

3 Protein, fat, carbohydrates and mineral salts.

4 Milk could provide enough energy and protein, but would be deficient in iron and vitamin B. In addition, it would not provide any roughage.

124 Nutrition

5.5 Beri-beri

1 Beri-beri could be caused by a nutritional deficiency in the polished rice, or by the presence of some disease-causing substance in the rice.

2 Feed chickens other, nutritionally sound, food left over from the meals of beri-beri patients. Allow physical contact between the patients and the chickens while giving the chickens a different diet. See if an afflicted chicken could pass on the disease. According to Eijkman all these courses of action should result in beri-beri appearing in the chickens. On the other hand, chickens could be fed a good diet as well as scraps from the patients, and on Eijkman's hypothesis they would not recover.

3 That beri-beri is infectious.

4 The incidence of beri-beri seems, on these figures, to be related to the type of rice diet. If it were infectious one would expect the figures to be different.

Vitamin B_1 was isolated from rice polishings in 1925 by Jansen and Donath in Java.

5.6 Fluoride and tooth decay

2 The figures come from a survey of over 7000 American children aged twelve to fourteen years from twenty-one cities. In order to present evidence such as this the main-points are that the people surveyed should be those most obviously affected by fluoride (children), the sample should be large, and data should be collected from many different places.

3 There is a marked inverse correlation between the amount of fluoride and tooth decay where the fluoride is present in amounts of less than one part per million. Thereafter, increases give only a small improvement.

4 For discussion, but a presumably 'natural rights' also include the right to fall sick from every water-borne disease, at present prevented by the removal of some things from water and the addition of others before it reaches our taps; b food provides a certain amount of fluoride, and in some areas the water already contains more than the 1 ppm proposed as an addition.

5 Yes. But could one be sure that all parents, except those who consciously opted out, would give their children the tablets?

5.7 The production of veal

1,2 a Loss of blood reduced the amount of haemoglobin in the body, and paler flesh was expected. The blood loss was, of course, fairly quickly made up by the calf.

b More milk drunk meant faster growth.

c Grass, but not milk, contains enough iron, and allows vitamin B_{12} to be made in the rumen. Both of these are necessary for the formation of haemoglobin.

d As plants which are grown in the dark are paler in colour than those grown in the light it was thought that animals reared in darkness would show a similar paleness. Darkness may, of course, discourage movement and keep the animals quiet, hence reinforcing **e**. It also discourages flies.

e If the calves were still they were using very little food in producing energy for movement. The formation of myoglobin was also hindered. Short tethering, or being tightly confined between bars, also stopped the calves licking urine which contains a little iron.

f, g The calves would become thirsty and would drink more milk at feed times.

h, i Both straw and ungalvanised iron objects would provide iron.

The next questions are best dealt with by discussion.

3 It is possible to call cruel all practices which do not let animals live as they would in the wild. An extreme view would then say that keeping any animals for food is unnatural, although many farm animals would not now last long in the wild. 'Nature' itself may well be more 'cruel' than any farm. From our point of view, many people may go hungry if the intensive production of farm animals is not developed.

4 Does the animal suffer from ill-health, does the treatment cause pain, does it affect the animal's natural functions?

5 Is loss or gain in mass in man connected with happiness or unhappiness?

6 Digestion

6.1 Control of gastric secretion
A   1, 3b, 4, 5.
B   2.
C   i   4, 5a, 6.
     ii   3b, 4, 5a.
D   i   4, 5, 7.
     ii   3a.
E   1, 3, 4, 5, 7c.
F   7a, 7b.
G   7c, 4, 5.
H   8.

6.2 Control of pancreatic secretion
The secretion of pancreatic juice is primarily controlled by hormones (intestinal phase), although there is a weaker neural regulation through the vagus nerve (cephalic phase). The hormones which act on the pancreas are produced by the intestine in response to the presence in it of acid or digestion products. The two major hormones are secretin which causes copious secretion of a very alkaline pancreatic juice poor in enzymes, and pancreomyzin which causes secretion of pancreatic juice rich in enzymes.

6.3 The digestion and absorption of fat
1   A water-soluble compound would dissolve in the intestinal mucosa and pass through the cells to the blood more easily. A fat droplet has to be small enough to be absorbed without going into solution. Fats, if sufficiently finely emulsified, can be absorbed directly without previous digestion.

2   There is no increase in the amount of oleic acid absorbed when glycerol or phosphate are added singly. When both are added together the amount absorbed is nearly twice as much as without the two. When the glycerol and phosphate are introduced as a compound, glyceryl phosphate, the amount absorbed is again increased.

3   There is no absorption when iodoacetate is added.

6.4 Digestion of cellulose

1 The flagellates produce glucose from cellulose by means of the enzyme cellulase. In fact, particles of wood are engulfed into the protozoan and digested, metabolism is anaerobic. In another termite family the organisms which digest the cellulose are bacteria.

2 It may be called a symbiotic relationship.

3 It seems not to be a symbiotic relationship, unless there are so few protozoa that their absence makes little difference. It could be commensalism, or, on the information given, the protozoa could even be parasitic.

6.5 Structure and function of the intestine and alveoli

1 a The intestine secretes mucus via the goblet cells, and enzymes via the crypts of Lieberkühn in the small intestine.

b The intestine has a very large internal surface area produced by folds and villi. There are about 20 to 40 villi per square millimetre, each 0.5 to 1 mm long. In addition, the free edges of the epithelial cells of the villi are divided into minute microvilli. The intestine is also very long. In man the duodenum is about 22 cm, and the jejunum and ileum about 258 cm. The total absorptive area is about 300 square metres.

There are smooth muscle fibres in the villi which enable them to move and thus come into contact with more digested food: during digestion the villi are in constant motion. There is a rich supply of blood vessels into which the products of digestion pass, particularly in the villi where the vessels form a network below the epithelium. The epithelial cells have a lot of mitochondria in them, associated with respiratory activity, and also pinocytic vesicles which absorb fat droplets.

c Peristalsis occurs by contraction of the circular and longitudinal muscle layers of the intestine.

2 The alveoli, like the infoldings of the intestine, give a large surface area, but unlike the intestine wall, that of the alveolus is very thin consisting of flattened cells which provide a very short distance for gases to pass through. The alveolar epithelial cells do not play an active part in absorption as do the intestinal epithelial cells. There is a rich blood supply, as in the intestine, in which the gases are carried. There is no muscle tissue, but the walls of the alveoli have some elastic fibres. The lining of the alveoli is wet and the gases dissolve in the liquid.

128 Digestion

6.6 Enzyme action under different conditions

1 $34\,°C$, pH 7.2.
2 Yes. The rate of reaction doubles for a rise of $10\,°C$.
3 The enzyme, a protein, is denatured.
4 **A:** an amylase, working best in neutral to slightly alkaline conditions.
   B: pepsin, in acid conditions in the stomach.
5 It could be the amount of enzyme available for reaction with the substrate, or the inhibition of the enzyme by an excess of substrate or product, or the maximum rate for that temperature.
6 **A:** enzyme concentration. Given enough substrate and no inhibition of the enzyme by the products of the reaction, the rate of reaction is directly proportional to the concentration of the enzyme present.
   B: time. The reaction starts when the enzyme is added to the substrate. At first the curve is nearly linear, but the rate then slows. The changes which affect the enzyme's activity are the accumulation of products which — if the reaction is reversible — may oppose the initial reaction, the reducing concentration of the substrate, and any pH change which may occur.

6.7 An enzyme experiment

1 E, which contains the most of both catalysts.
2 D, E. The enzyme will be destroyed at $60\,°C$, but not the metallic catalyst. D and E contain twice as much catalyst as B.
3 D, E. The enzyme will be affected in C and B.
4 E. Increasing the substrate concentration will increase the rate of reaction.
5 All flasks.
6 All flasks.

6.8 The liver and blood sugar

1 The animal is able to convert carnivorous food substances in its diet to sugar.
2 Something happens to the blood as it passes through the liver, causing an increase in its sugar concentration. There is no evidence yet that the liver adds sugar to the blood.
3 The liver does not act directly on the blood, disproving the belief held in Bernard's time. Fresh liver contains sugar which can be removed by

washing, and also contains another substance, which Bernard called glycogen (sugar former). This remains in the liver during the washing, and can later be changed to sugar.

4 It seems to be an enzyme action.

5 a   b   c, g   d   e, f   d, e, f.

6.9 Diabetes

1 The excess glucose could be stored and used later.

2 To get down to the minimum blood sugar level. Food or drink would raise the level and interfere with the readings during the test.

3 Too little. The blood glucose goes up to high levels and drops slowly.

4 a Remove the pancreas and see if diabetes follows.

   b Macerate the Islet tissue, filter, use the filtrate to inject into a diabetic animal. Any internal secretion produced by the Islet cells will still be present in the filtrate and should act on the blood sugar.

   c Inject insulin into an animal without a pancreas and see if the diabetic condition is improved.

   d Ligature the pancreatic duct, this should have no effect on blood sugar levels.

5 The protein digesting enzyme in the pancreas destroys the protein insulin.

7 Nerves and Muscles

7.1 Conduction in nerves
I   A - 3.   B - 1.   C - 4.   D - 2.

II   5   The evidence given implies that the impulse gets the energy locally as it goes along. Indeed, it seems that conduction in a part of the nerve can be determined by local conditions there, such as a low temperature.

     6   a   The whole preparation does not behave in an all or nothing way, but
           b   the individual fibres give an all or nothing response, although each may have a different threshold. As each threshold is reached there is an increase in muscle contraction. In a nerve with a lot of fibres it is impossible to detect this.
           c   Once threshold is reached, the action potential does not vary.

III   7   The similarities would also support the hypothesis that the impulse is a chemical reaction which is accompanied by an electrical change. The action potential would then be simply the manifestation of the process, like the noise of an engine.

     8   The speed of conduction, which is too fast for a chemical process depending on diffusion. Also, electric currents externally applied to a nerve cause muscle contraction, and the action potential produces an electric current.

7.2 Nerve-muscle preparations
1 See Fig. 61.

Fig. 61. **Record of a single muscle twitch**

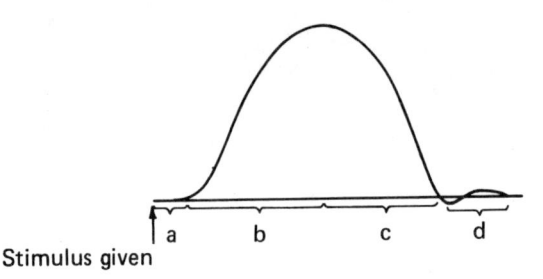

Stimulus given   a   b   c   d

2. See Fig. 62.

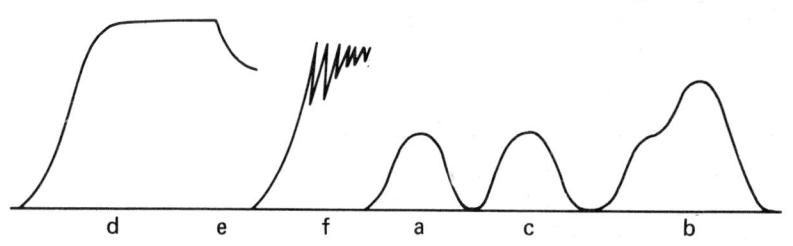

Fig. 62. Diagrams of muscle twitch tracings

d   e   f   a   c   b

3 Curve A is at 10 °C. At this temperature a rise of 10 °C about doubles the speed of contraction, shortening the latent period. It also gives a higher tracing.

7.3 Neuromuscular transmission

1 is supported by **A, B, C** and **E**.

2 is supported by **A, D** and **E**.

Curare acts by making the muscle cell membrane at the end plate insensitive to acetyl choline. Acetyl choline is still released at the end plates but no depolarisation follows.

7.4 Reflexes

1 When the cut part of the ventral root going to the body is stimulated there is muscular contraction, indicating that the ventral root is a motor nerve. Neither part of the cut ventral root contains sensory fibres. Stimulating the dorsal root going to the body causes no muscular action, indicating the absence of motor fibres. Pain is caused by stimulating the other cut end, indicating sensory fibres. This stimulus also causes muscular contraction, indicating a connection inside the cord.

2 By the time the sound and food have been given together 30 times, the conditioned reflex is established, both in extent and length of latent period (third column). Even after twenty times, there is a considerable response.

3 For discussion. It is tempting to extrapolate when one sees that some people, constantly having to make fine discriminations — although not about meals — may show signs of stress or bad temper.

132 Nerves and Muscles

7.5 Muscle contraction

1 The thick filaments are made of myosin, the thinner ones of actin. The thicker ones constitute 35 per cent of the total protein, the thinner ones only 15 per cent.

2 Yes.

3 The A band stays the same, the H and I bands get shorter.

4 During contraction there is no change in the length of the A band, so the filaments of myosin which constitute the A band remain the same length, and neither set of filaments coils or folds. This suggests that the shortening is due to the thinner filaments moving between the myosin filaments towards each other, thus shortening the H band.

5 Six times in each half of the sarcomere.

7.6 Glycolysis in muscle

1 A is supported by **2, 3, 5.**
   B is supported by **1, 2, 4.**
   C is supported by **2, 3, 5.**
   D is supported by **4.**
   E is supported by **2, 3. 5.**

7.7 Rods and cones

1 Rods. Some mammals, for example, bats, hedgehogs, whales, have retinas which contain only rods.

2 The blind spot.

3 Cones, which work well in bright light, coincide with greatest acuity of vision in the light-adapted eye. There are cones only in the fovea. Relative visual acuity in the dark-adapted eye corresponds with the distribution of rods.

4 a The light-adapted eye   b the dark-adapted eye.

5 i   a   iv c   vii f
   ii a   v d, e   viii g, c
   iii a, b   vi d   ix a, d, e, g

6 While wearing red goggles they can still see in bright light, but as the light falling on the eye is red, the rods are stimulated very little and behave as though they were already in dim light, thus becoming dark-adapted.